# CHRISTIAN

## LOVE

# CHRISTIAN

## FORGIVENESS

## By Robert Eldredge Sr.

CHOICE
PUBLICATIONS

Unless otherwise indicated, all Scripture quotations are from the King James Version of the Bible

Scripture taken from the Holy Bible, NIV. Copyright 1973,1978, 1984 by New York International Bible Society. Used by permission of Zondervan Corporation. All rights reserved.

Cover design by Joseph Eldredge

Cover image featuring *The Virgin and Child with Saint Anne* by Leonardo Da Vinci, courtesy of the Google Art Project

Set in arial font,

**ISBN - 979-8-9882132-2-2**

# C O N T E N T S

## Part 2                 It's All about Love

## Part 3                 The Root of Bitterness

## Appendix                 194

# FORWARD

In the counseling of married or divorced couples, it became apparent to me that their lack of forgiveness and genuine love for one another was usually the main cause of their inability to communicate and reconcile their differences. Of course, this same unforgiveness and lack of love can also apply to other relationships as well, so I am also including some excerpts from my previous book, Christian Divorce Christian Remarriage.

You will find that this book is divided into three parts:

God's Love and Forgiveness

It's All about Love

The Root of Bitterness

With this book, I hope to teach you three things:

First, you can be friends with God. God is love. Through God's love, we can love. Through love, you can be free from all anger and depression.

Second, Jesus is the way to God's love. Jesus is our eternal high priest. Through Him and his intercession, you can love and forgive your own self, and love and forgive others, even your enemies. Love increases with forgiveness.

Third, I want to tell you how a 'Root of Bitterness' begins and its consequences. There is no bitterness in love. Through love, God is preparing us for eternity.

Reader, I want to invite you into the greatest gift you could ever receive, a life that is full of Christian Love and Forgiveness!

# Part I

## God's Love and Forgiveness

Wouldn't you like to be *friends* with our God and our Lord instead of just being his *servants*?

And it is relatively easy to do for we are now living in the Age of Grace where all sins are forgivable. All you have to do to become His *friend* is to receive his Son, Jesus Christ, as your own Lord and Savior and then do whatsoever He inspires you to do.

"This is my commandment, That ye love one another, as I have loved you. Greater love hath no more than this, that a man lay down his life for his friends. Ye are my friends, if ye do whatsoever I command you. Henceforth I call you not servants; for the servant knoweth not what his lord doeth: but I have called you friends; for all things that I have heard of my Father I have made known unto you." (John 15:1215)

If you already love and believe in Jesus, then God the father will also love you. For Jesus has promised that,

"Because I live, you also will live. On that day you will realize that I am in my Father, and you are in me, and I am in you. Whoever has my commands and keeps them is the one who loves me. The one who loves me will be loved by my Father, and I too will love them and show myself to them." (John 14:19-21 NIV)

It's certainly a lot easier to love Jesus than to try to obey all 613 rules and instructions in the Law of Moses!

"Owe no man anything, but to love one another: for he that loveth another hath fulfilled the law. For this, Thou shalt not commit adultery, Thou shalt not kill, Thou shalt not steal, Thou shalt not bear false witness, Thou shalt not covet; and if there be any other commandment, it is briefly com-prehended in this saying, namely, Thou shalt love thy neighbor as thyself." (Romans 13:8-9)

### The Love of Jesus

Shortly before Jesus was to suffer and die upon the cross as a substitute for all our sins, He gave to his disciples "a new commandment" that they were to "love one another as He had loved them." He also added that their love for one another would be how people would know that they were His disciples.

"A new commandment I give unto you, that ye love one another; as I have loved you, that ye also love one another. By this shall all men know that ye are my disciples, if ye have love one to another." (John 13: 34-35)

Then after Jesus was resurrected from the dead and been given all authority over heaven and earth, He instructed His disciples to go into all the earth and "make disciples of all nations." They were also told to baptize believers in the name of the Father, Son, and the Holy Spirit" and to teach them "to obey everything I have commanded you."

"Then Jesus came to them and said, All authority in heaven and on earth has been given to me. Therefore go and make disciples of all nations, baptizing them in the name of the Father and of the Son and of the Holy Spirit, and teaching them to obey everything I have commanded you." (Matthew 28:18-20 NIV)

Although we are all saved and justified by the grace of God through our faith in the sacrifice of His only begotten Son, a true evangelistic message should also include our Lord's higher calling to true discipleship and a greater degree of intimacy with Him.

Of course, this also includes loving one another and obeying everything that our Lord has commanded. And if we would all love one another with the pure and the unselfish love of Jesus Christ, then there would never be a problem with unforgiveness. For how could anyone withhold forgiveness from those whom they really loved with all of their heart?

That's why we still need Jesus.

Jesus knew that no human being could ever equal or even approach the extremely high level of His own love and sacrifice. But Jesus also knew that His disciples would soon be "born again" after He died and rose again and that they would become entirely new creations when they received His overcoming Spirit.

"So from now on we regard no one from a worldly point of view. Though we once regarded Christ in this way, we do so no longer. Therefore, if anyone is in Christ, the new creation has come: The old has gone, the new is here! All this is from God, who reconciled us to Himself through Christ and gave us the ministry of reconciliation" (2 Corinthians 5:1618 NIV)

His disciples probably first became new creations when they became believers and the resurrected Jesus breathed upon them and imparted His Holy Spirit.

Again Jesus said, "Peace be with you! As the Father has sent me, I am sending you." And with that He breathed on them and said, "Receive the Holy spirit. " (John 20.01-22 NIV)

Jesus also knew that shortly after they had received the Spirit of Christ "within" them, that they would also be empowered even further when the Holy Spirit would come "upon" them on the day of Pentecost.

"He said to them: "It is not for you to know the times or dates the Father has set by his own authority. But you will receive power when the Holy Spirit comes on you; and you will be my witnesses in Jerusalem, and in all Judea and Samaria, and to the ends of the earth. " (Acts 1:7-8 NIV)

Although the Holy Spirit was also helpful in making them more like Jesus, the primary purpose of the Holy Spirit coming "upon" the disciples was to enable them to have the ability to be bold witnesses of the love of God throughout all the earth and to confirm the Word of God "with signs following."

"And they went forth, and preached everywhere, the Lord working with them, and confirming the word with signs following. Amen. " (Mark 16:20)

"When we abide in and obey the promptings of the Spirit of Christ within us to love one another, this is what will transform us from glory to glory to be more and more like our Lord." (2 Corinthians 3:17-18)

God is Love, so He gave us Jesus.

God is the personification of Love so "whoever does not love does not know God, because God is love." He already wants to forgive us even though we have all sinned and transgressed against His holy and righteous commandments. And God's perfect justice has already been satisfied by the sacrificial death and the resurrection of his only begotten Son, Jesus Christ, so our sinfulness is no longer the issue.

"Dear friends, let us love one another, for love comes from God. Everyone who loves has been born of God and knows God. Whoever does not love does not know God, because God is love. This is how God showed his love among us: He sent his one and only Son into the world that we might live through him. (1 John 4:7-9 NW)

Like the father of the prodigal son, the only thing that God is waiting for now is genuine repentance so that you can receive His love and forgiveness and acknowledge that His only begotten Son has already paid the price for your redemption.

"The Lord is not slack concerning His promise, as some men count slackness; but is longsuffering to usward, not willing that any should perish, but that all should come to repentance." (2 Peter 3:9)

The Law that was given by Moses    was good for that particular time as its commandments were helpful in restraining the evils of those days. But we are now living in the Age of Grace (unmerited favor) under a new and a much better covenant, for "grace and truth came by Jesus Christ."

"And of His fullness have all we received, and grace for grace. For the law was given by Moses, but grace and truth came by Jesus Christ." (John 1:16-17)

The 613 strict rules and precepts in the Law of Moses, and even the ultimate sacrifice of His only begotten Son, have made some people think that our Creator must be a very harsh and an unloving God, but this is simply not true.

The sacrifice of His only begotten Son was only to satisfy the perfect righteousness of God so that we could receive by grace (unmerited favor) a far better love covenant relationship with Him. And this New Covenant of grace reveals the goodness of God and just how much He really does love us and already wants to forgive us all of our sins.

"But now hath He obtained a more excellent ministry, by how much also He is the mediator of a better covenant, which was established upon better promises. For if that first covenant had been faultless, then should no place have been sought for the second." (Hebrews 8:6-7)

The unconditional love and the forgiveness of our heavenly Father for the repentant sinner are probably best expressed in the parable of the prodigal son in the fifteenth chapter of the book of Luke.

Even though the son had foolishly wasted his entire inheritance on sinful living, he decided to go back home because he knew he would be much better off even if he was only one of his father's servants.

When the son did return home, his father saw him from afar off and ran to meet him. He welcomed the return of his son with great rejoicing and immediately gave him his best robe and a ring for his finger. Then he prepared a big feast to celebrate his return. This is how much our own heavenly Father also loves us.

"And he arose and came to his father. But when he was yet a great way off, his father saw him, and had compassion, and ran, and fell on his neck, and kissed him. And the son said unto him, Father, I have sinned against heaven, and in thy sight, and am no more worthy to be called thy son. But the father said to his servants, Bring forth the best robe, and put it on him; and put a ring on his hand, and shoes on his feet: And bring hither the fatted calf, and kill it; and let us eat, and be merry: For this my son was dead, and is alive again; he was lost, and is found. And they began to be merry." (Luke 20-24)


## Christ's Nature


The word "Christ" is *not* the last name of Jesus. It is in fact Greek for the Hebrew word "mashiyach" which is translated as "Messiah", and both words literally mean "the anointed one" or "the anointing."

Jesus had revealed that He had no beginning and no end when He said, "I tell you the truth, before Abraham was born, I AM", (John 8:58) so it was clearly understood at that time that Jesus was claiming to be the promised Jewish Messiah.

Most Christian believers can relate to Jesus as the humble suffering servant, but many cannot relate to His Father or even to Jesus as He is now, the Lord over all the earth as its regal King of Kings.

But Jesus already told us that "He that hath seen me hath seen the Father" and that 'the Father and I are one" so they both must have the same nature and attributes.

"Jesus saith unto him, Have I been so long time with you, and yet hast thou not known me, Philip? He that hath seen me hath seen the Father; and how sayest thou then, Show us the Father? Believest thou not that I am in the Father, and the Father in me? The words that I speak unto you I speak not of myself, but the Father that dwelleth in me, He doeth the works." (John 14: 9-10)

The "oneness" of God was also confirmed in the Jewish Schema, which says, "Hear O Israel, the Lord our God is one Lord." (Deuteronomy 6:4, Mark 12:29) And the Nicene Creed confirmed in 325 AD that, although they can act independently, the three persons in our Triune God are united together as "one" and are of "one substance."

If you should still feel that our heavenly Father is not a loving and caring God, then it may help for you to know that both the Father and the Son suffered together when the body of Jesus was on the cross, for "God was in Christ, reconciling the world unto Himself."

"And all things are of God, who hath reconciled us to Himself by Jesus Christ, and hath given to us the ministry of reconciliation; To wit, that God was in Christ, reconciling the world unto Himself, not imputing their trespasses unto them; and hath committed unto us the word of reconciliation." (2 Corinthians 5:18-19)

His righteous wrath was therefore really upon the inherited sins and the iniquities of the entire human race that were passed down from Adam and Eve and others, both now and in the future. These are what our Lord took on when He became a man. (John 1: 14)

God's wrath was never upon His only begotten Son, whom He repeatedly said that He greatly loved. So how could His Father not also suffer greatly when He had to allow his own beloved Son, whom He dearly loved, suffer from so much pain and evil acts?

"And Jesus, when He was baptized, went up straightway out of the water: and the heavens were opened unto Him, and He saw the Spirit of God descending like a dove, and lighting upon Him: And a voice from heaven, saying, This is my beloved Son, in whom I am well pleased." (Matthew 3:16-17)

This was actually how the prophecy predicted in the book of Genesis was fulfilled by God through the "seed of the woman", and how Satan's evil plans were defeated so that all mankind could be redeemed and blessed with the blessings that God had intended for all mankind. (Genesis 3:14-15)

This plan was kept secret, for God knew that if the princes of this world knew it, 'they would not have crucified the Lord of Glory." And He may have some other secrets that He does not want Satan to know...

"But we speak the wisdom of God in a mystery, even the hidden wisdom, which God ordained before the world unto our glory: Which none of the princes of this world knew: for had they known it, they would not have crucified the Lord of glory." (1 Corinthians 2:7-8)

Yes, God does sometimes gets angry and does at times even have righteous wrath, but it is always because of some great evil or injustice. And He has warned us that, like most lovers, He is a "jealous God" so his wrath will be upon those who hate Him, but his love and mercy will be upon all who love Him.

"Thou shalt not bow down thy self to them, nor serve them: for I the Lord thy God am a jealous God, visiting the iniquity of the fathers upon the children unto the third and fourth generation of them that hate me; And showing mercy unto thousands of them that love me, and keep my commandments." (Exodus 20: 5-6)

He was certainly angry when Lucifer, who was the worship leader in heaven, wanted to be worshipped himself and even tried to start his own kingdom with one third of God's angels, so God in His wrath cast them all out of His perfect Heaven.

He was also angry and deeply saddened when Adam and Eve, who were made in His own image, believed Satan's lie that God had evil intent when He was keeping the knowledge of good and evil from them.

God would obviously have preferred that they would not have failed their simple test, but He still loved them so He had already made contingency plans for their redemption as well as for all their descendants who would also fail their tests.

And yet He allowed us all to be tested and tempted by Satan, for He knew that when we were eventually forgiven because of the sacrifice of His Son, that our love for Him would be just that much greater.

"Wherefore I say unto thee, her sins, which are many, are forgiven; for she loved much: but to whom little is forgiven, the same loveth little." (Luke 7:47)

## Baptism was for the Repentant

Water baptism by immersion was not new, for it was also practiced by other religions. And the Jews were already baptizing their proselytes to their faith. But "John the Baptist" added a new dimension as he was ordained to "prepare the way for the Lord" by getting people to repent of their sins and "make straight the paths" for the much greater ministry of Jesus Christ.

"In those days John the Baptist came, preaching in the wilderness of Judea and saying, 'Repent, for the kingdom of heaven has come near. ' This is he who was spoken of through the prophet Isaiah."

"A voice of one calling in the wilderness, 'Prepare the way for the Lord, make straight the paths for him." (Matthew 3:13, Isaiah 40:3 NIV)

And Jesus also began his own ministry with the very same admonition for people to "Repent, for the kingdom of heaven has come near." The Jews, and later the Gentiles, had to repent so that they could believe the good news that the kingdom of heaven had now come near.

"From that time on Jesus began to preach, "Repent, for the kingdom of heaven has come near." (Matthew 4:17 NIV)

What John the Baptist was doing by getting people to repent must have been a very important ministry, for Jesus said that there was no man born of woman who was greater than John the Baptist.

"Verily I say unto you, Among them that are born of women: notwithstanding he that is least in the kingdom of heaven is greater than he." (Matthew 11:11)

And the prodigal son would have never known the love of his earthly father if he had not repented of his former lifestyle and wisely decided to return home. In like manner, we should also have at least a strong desire to stop our bad behavior before asking our heavenly Father for his forgiveness.

God is merciful, but we should have both repentance and remorse for our sins in order to be totally free. When someone refuses to stop his or her offensive behavior, we should rebuke them but not judge or condemn them.

"If thy brother trespass against thee, rebuke him; and if he repents, forgive him. And trespass against thee seven times in a day, and seven times in a day turn again to thee, saying I repent; thou shalt forgive him." (Luke 17:3-4)

The general rule is that we should always forgive anyone who repents. And even if they do not repent, our own love and the love of God and his "kindness, forbearance and patience" is normally the best way to lead a person to repentance.

"So when you, a mere human being, pass judgment on them and yet do the same things, do you think you will escape God's judgment? Or do you show contempt for the riches of His kindness, forbearance and patience, not realizing that God's kindness is intended to lead you to repentance?" (Romans 2:3-4)

And yet there is even an exception to this general rule mentioned in the fifth Chapter of Paul's first letter to the Corinthians. The sin of incest was so heinous that Paul requested that the man be removed from all church fellowship and activities until he repented so that his eternal soul "may be saved."

"In the name of our Lord Jesus Christ, when ye are gathered together, and my spirit, with the power of our Lord Jesus Christ, to deliver such an one unto Satan for the destruction of the flesh, that the spirit may be saved in the day of the Lord Jesus." (1 Corinthians 5:4-5)

And yet the Lord's forgiveness even for the sin of incest was expressed in Paul's second letter to the Corinthians. Apparently, the man had repented and stopped his incestual relationship, so Paul advised the church to forgive him, restore him back into full fellowship, and "to reaffirm your love for him."

"The punishment inflicted on him by the majority is sufficient. Now instead, you ought to forgive and comfort him, so that he will not be overwhelmed by excessive sorrow. I urge you, therefore, to rearm your love for him." (2 Corinthians 2:6-8 NIV)

I once met with Basilea Schlink who told us privately how she was led by the Lord to start her ministry in Darmstadt, Germany. Later, she wrote an excellent book entitled, "Repentance - The Joy Filled Life", and her peaceful demeanor and the joy that could be easily seen on her face was ample proof that she was practicing what she preached.

The original Greek word (metanoeo) translated as "repent" literally means "to have another mind." And that other mind could refer simply to the changing of our own mind, but it could also refer to the mind of Christ that you receive when you become a believer.

Because of the fallen nature of mankind, the mind of Christ is quite different from the mind of the average man and woman. We all tend to look favorably at those who exercise dominion over others; and look less favorably upon those who are humble servants. But Jesus said that "whosoever will be great among you, let him be your minister. And whosoever will be chief among you, let him be your servant."

"But Jesus called them unto him, and said, Ye know that the princes of the Gentiles exercise dominion over them, and they that are great exercise authority upon them. But it shall not be so among you: but whosoever will be great among you, let him be your minister; And whosoever will be chief among you, let him be your servant: Even as the Son of man came not to be ministered unto, but to minister, and to give His life a ransom for many." (Matthew 20:25-28)

Water baptism now has a different meaning today, for Jesus has already fulfilled the purpose of John's baptism and the Kingdom of God has now become available to all believers.

The purpose of water baptism is now to "die" to our old selfish carnal nature and yield to the new mind of Christ within us that we receive when we become believers in Jesus. This is so that we can put our faith and trust in the grace and the mercy of our Lord and not upon the futility of our own inadequate works.

"And he said unto them, Unto what then were ye baptized? And they said, Unto John's baptism. Then said Paul, John verily baptized with the baptism of repentance, saying unto the people, that they should believe on him which should come after him, that is, on Christ Jesus. When they heard this, they were baptized in the name of the Lord Jesus." (Acts 19:35)

Even in Paul's days, there were some who questioned whether we were really saved by grace through faith and not by our own works. Some believers were apparently still skeptical for they either said or thought: "Shall we continue in sin, that grace may abound?" and Paul answered as follows:

"What shall we say then? Shall we continue in sin, that grace may abound? God forbid. How shall we, that are dead to sin, live any longer therein? Know ye not, that so many of us as were baptized into Jesus Christ were baptized into his death? Therefore, we are buried with him by baptism into death: that like as Christ was raised up from the dead by the glory of the Father, even so we also should walk in newness of life." (Romans 6:2-4)

If you are already a spiritually reborn Christian, then it should be a lot easier to love and forgive others for "the mind of Christ" now dwells within your human spirit. Of course, even if you are not yet a believer in Jesus Christ, you can and should still forgive others even if it is only for your own peace of mind.

"But the natural man receiveth not the things of the Spirit of God: for they are foolishness unto him: neither can he know them, because they are spiritually discerned. But he that is spiritual judgeth all things, yet he himself is judged of no man. For who hath known the mind of the Lord, that he may instruct him? But we have the mind of Christ." (1 Corinthians 2:14-16)

And don't forget that whenever you forgive someone, this does not mean that you are approving of that person's past or present behavior. When you yield your mind to the mind of Christ, you will always forgive others, but the Lord's own words will still be the judge of that person's behavior if he or she does not repent before they die.

"I am come a light into the world, that whosoever believeth on me should not abide in darkness. And if any man hear my words, and believe not, I judge him not: for I came not to judge the world, but to save the world. He that rejecteth me, and receiveth not my words, hath one that judgeth him: the word that I have spoken, the same shall judge him in the last day." (John 12:46-48)

In some cases, forgiveness may not be applicable as there appears to be no repentance at all, but your love for them will always be applicable. So even if some refuse to repent, you should still continue to pray for God to forgive them and treat them with genuine love, kindness, and respect.

"Brethren, if a man be overtaken in a fault, ye which are spiritual, restore such an one in the spirit of meekness; considering thyself, lest thou also be tempted." (Galatians 6: 1)

When Jesus was dying on the cross, He prayed for his heavenly Father to forgive even those who were crucifying Him for "they know not what they do." Since they were obviously unrepentant, we can also use this prayer for others who refuse to repent, for they also "know not what they do." (Luke 23:34)

## Forgiveness is an Act of Love

Forgiveness is an act of love, and the greatest act of love in the entire universe was that of Jesus who was already "in the form of God," but He voluntarily took upon Himself the sins of all humanity "and became obedient unto death, even the death of the cross," so that we might all be forgiven of our sins.

"Let this mind be in you, which was also in Christ Jesus: Who, being in the form of God, thought it not robbery to be equal with God: But made Himself of no reputation, and took upon Him the form of a servant, and was made in the likeness of men: And being found in fashion as a man, He humbled Himself, and became obedient unto death, even the death of the cross." (Philippians 2:5-8)

The definition of this unselfish "agape" kind of love that only comes from God was originally defined by the apostle Paul in the following Scripture.

"Love [agape] is patient, love is kind. It does not envy, it does not boast, it is not proud. It is not rude, it is not self-seeking, it is not easily angered, it keeps no records of wrongs. Love does not delight in evil but rejoices with the truth. It always protects, always trusts, always hopes, always perseveres." (I Corinthians 13:4-7 NIV)

Therefore, if you love someone with this godly kind of love, you will be "kind" and "not easily angered." And perhaps the most important of all, you will also forgive that person who has offended you and "keep no records of wrongs."

To forgive is an act of love that should always be followed up with a firm decision to just "let it go" and forget about it. You should not even bring up the past offenses again unless there is a very good reason for doing so. And if you will forgive from your heart, then it will be just as if the offenses had never even happened!

"Above all, love each other deeply, because love covers over a multitude of sins." (1 Peter 4:8 NIV)

Since God is very merciful to us under our new and much better covenant of Grace and will not bring up again our own past sins and iniquities, then we should also show the same mercy for each other. In other words, if we should all practice what is called the "golden rule" then we will not only forgive, but we could even become very close friends.

"So in everything, do to others what you would have them do to you, for this sums up the Law and the Prophets." (Matthew 7:12 NIV)

And don't forget that Jesus loves and died for all, so if you have already been forgiven of your own sins, then it is even more important that you should forgive others as well and "remember no more" their sins and iniquities.

"And they shall not teach every man his neighbor, and every man his brother, saying, Know the Lord: for all shall know me, from the least to the greatest. For I will be merciful to their unrighteousness, and their sins and their iniquities will I remember no more." (Hebrews 8:11-12)

When you really love Jesus, you will automatically want to obey His teachings. Then is heavenly Father will love you and they both will come to you and make their home within you. Your physical body is then considered holy for it is the tabernacle of God.

"Jesus replied, "Anyone who loves me will obey my teaching. My Father will love them, and we will come to them and make our home with them. Anyone who does not love me will not obey my teaching. These words you hear are not my own; they belong to the Father who sent me." (John 14:23-24 NIV)

Forgiveness adds no conditions.

Forgiveness is a choice, both to give and to receive forgiveness. The word translated "forgive" comes from the Greek word "aphiemi" which means "to send away."

We are all imperfect human beings, and we all make mistakes, so the key to happiness and contentment is really not how much we know, but rather how much we can forgive and then "send away" from the thoughts in our minds.

Once there has been repentance and forgiveness by our very holy God, then our forgiveness should have no other conditions.

Therefore, you should never add on any extra conditions such as that they must first "admit they were wrong" or "say they are sorry" or make any other requirements before you will agree to forgive them.

Adding any conditions for your forgiveness would be the equivalent of emotional blackmail and can be guaranteed to result in a lack of 'true' repentance even if they should agree to do what you request.

So if you are still withholding your forgiveness until there is compliance to some unjust demands, you will only end up by condemning yourself, for you will ultimately be judged by God.

The much more severe judgment of God would be only upon the person who refuses to forgive and certainly not be upon the person who has already repented and been forgiven by God.

"If we confess our sins, He is faithful and just to forgive us our sins, and to cleanse us from all unrighteousness." (1 John 1:9)

Human forgiveness is helpful but not necessary once having been forgiven by God, so we should never have to plead or 'beg' for forgiveness. The common misconception that we "must be forgiven by those we have offended" has been falsely perpetuated in Christian circles mostly because of a combination of the selfish desire for revenge by the forgiver and/or the feelings of guilt and shame by the offender.

You can and should apologize in order to express your regret or remorse for anything you might have done that offended another person. And restitution should also be done whenever it is applicable. And if the offended person forgives you, then there can be genuine love for one another, and former relationships can once again be restored.

Most people who withhold their forgiveness do it selfishly in order to either justify themselves or their doctrinal positions. But in some cases, there are those who will do this in order to get revenge or even to torment the other person. This is a far greater evil and will result in even greater judgment from our holy and righteous God to come upon those who do this.

## Forgiveness Heals Us

Jesus pointed out to the skeptical Pharisees not only that the "Son of Man has the authority to forgive sins" but when He declared that a person's sins were forgiven, this had the same effect as saying that they were healed of various diseases.

"Some men brought to Him a paralyzed man, lying on a mat. When Jesus saw their faith, He said to the man, "Take heart, son; your sins are forgiven." At this, some of the teachers of the law said to themselves, "This fellow is blaspheming!" Knowing their thoughts, Jesus said, "Why do you entertain evil thoughts in your hearts? Which is easier to say, 'Your sins are forgiven',' or to say, 'Get up and walk'? But I want you to know that the Son of Man has authority on earth to forgive sins. " So He said to the paralyzed man, "Get up, take your mat and go home." (Matthew 9:2-6 NIV)

The disciples of Jesus were the first under our new covenant with God to receive the Spirit of Christ in their human spirit which was then "quickened" to be like Jesus. Previously under the old covenant, the Holy Spirit would only briefly abide upon the priest, prophet, or king and a few others in order to fulfill the special purposes of God.

"There is a natural body, and there is a spiritual body. And so it is written, The first man Adam was made a living soul; the last Adam (Jesus) was made a quickening spirit." (1 Corinthians 15:44-45)

And since the Spirit of Christ was now in them, they were given the same authority to forgive or retain sins that Jesus had. But it is still mind boggling to think that imperfect human beings could be given such authority while still living here on the earth!

"Again, Jesus said, "Peace be with you! As the Father has sent me, I am sending you. " And with that He breathed on them and said, "Receive the Holy Spirit. If you forgive anyone's sins, their sins are forgiven; if you do not forgive them, they are not forgiven." (John 20.01-23 NIV)

Therefore, all who are spiritually "born-again" today and have received the quick-ening Spirit of Christ in their hearts are "complete in Him" for we know that "in Him dwelleth all the fullness of the Godhead bodily."

"Beware lest any man spoil you through philosophy and vain deceit, after the tradition of men, after the rudiments of the world, and not after Christ. For in Him dwelleth all the fullness of the Godhead bodily. And ye are complete in Him, which is the head of all principality and power." (Colossians 2:8-10)

Now here is the awesome part. This must mean that all truly "born again" believers also have the same authority as Jesus and His disciples as long as they pray or speak under the unction (anointing) of the Holy Spirit. This is why it is even more important for all who have been "born again" to always forgive others.

It's important to think about those who have never repented, and to pray for them too and leave their final judgment up to God. Our forgiveness would not be complete without our own sincere repentance, even when others unremittently harm us. How do we do that?

The deacon Stephen had the answer as he was able to pray for those who were obviously unrepentant and were stoning him to death. After he prayed "Lord Jesus, receive my spirit," he then interceded for them all saying, "Lord, do not hold this sin against them."

I have since used this kind of a prayer for anyone who is or might be unrepentant (only God knows for sure.). And I also added a prayer that God would do whatever was necessary to bring them to repentance before they died so that their souls might be saved.

"When the members of the Sanhedrin heard this, they were furious and gnashed their teeth at him. But Stephen, full of the Holy Spirit, looked up to heaven and saw the glory of God, and Jesus standing at the right hand of God. "Look, " he said, "I see heaven open, and the Son of Man standing at the right hand of God." At this they covered their ears and, yelling at the top of their voices; they all rushed at him, dragged him out of the city and began to stone him. Meanwhile, the witnesses laid their coats at the feet of a young man named Saul. While they were stoning him, Stephen prayed, "Lord Jesus, receive my spirit. Then he fell on his knees and cried out, "Lord, do not hold this sin against them. " When he had said this, he fell asleep." (Acts 7:54-60 NIV)

Most Bible scholars believe that it was Stephen's merciful prayer that was responsible for extending the grace of God to the then unbelieving Saul (who was later renamed Paul) so that his soul could be saved and be supernaturally converted to Christianity while on the road to Damascus. (Acts 9:1-7)

At this particular time, Saul had no merit of his own, so he definitely needed the prayers and the mercy of God for he was still having many good Christians executed, beaten, or put into prison for "blasphemy."

If we haven't forgiven before we die, then it may be too late for God cannot allow any unforgiveness in His Kingdom. We are now living in the Age of Grace where all repented and confessed sins are forgivable, so there will be many in Heaven who have done some very terrible things and have been forgiven by God but must also be forgiven by their peers.

That is also why learning to forgive while on earth is so important. What do you think eternity would be like if we were not able to forgive and love one another? And worse yet, how would you feel if there were people in Heaven who knew you and would never forgive you for what *you* had done?

"Know ye not that the unrighteous shall not inherit the kingdom of God? Be not deceived: neither fornicators, nor idolaters, nor adulterers, nor effeminate, nor abusers of themselves with mankind, nor thieves, nor covetous, nor drunkards, nor revilers, nor extortioners, shall inherit the kingdom of God. And such were some of you: but ye are washed, but ye are sanctified, but ye are justified in the name of the Lord Jesus, and by the Spirit of our God." (I Corinthians 6.09-11)

Forgiving others will also be for our own good even while we are still on this earth, for we cannot have unforgiveness or bitterness in our hearts without the reaping of its spiritual consequences.

Remember this:

*Holding on to bitterness or unforgiveness is like drinking poison and then waiting for the other person to die.*

And if you have become a believer in Jesus Christ and have already been forgiven of all of your own sins and mistakes by the Grace and the Mercy of God, how could you *not* forgive those who have also sinned and made similar mistakes?

So, instead of focusing our thoughts upon the evil that may or not have happened in the past, we should just forgive everyone and "let it all go" and let God be the judge if any further action should be necessary, for He knows the thoughts and the intents of our hearts.

"Dearly beloved, avenge not yourselves, but rather give place unto wrath: for it is written, Vengeance is mine; I will repay, saith the Lord." (Romans 12:19)

Then we can focus our thoughts upon the good things in this world that our God is doing and spend our time in actually doing the works of God and praising and worshipping Him for His love and goodness.

And if you should do this and forgive one another, then "the God of peace shall be with you" and you will have His peace abundantly in your hearts.

"Finally, brethren, whatsoever things are true, whatsoever things are honest, whatsoever things are just, whatsoever things are pure, whatsoever things are lovely, whatsoever things are of good report; if there be any virtue, and if there be any praise, think on these things. Those things, which ye have both learned, and received, and heard, and seen in me, do. and the God of peace shall be with you." (Philippians 4:8-9)

## Unforgiveness is Selfishness

Unforgiveness is self imposed bondage for it has severe consequences even if it should not be openly expressed. Unforgiveness is also rebellion against the perfect will of God, for He wants us all to be conformed to the image of His only begotten Son.

In the parable of the prodigal son, the extreme selfishness and the complete lack of love exhibited by the elder brother is fully revealed. His reaction was the exact opposite of the unconditional love that was shown by his own father.

- The elder brother was self-centered. His entire world was centered on himself, so he really did not care that his long-lost brother had finally been found safe and sound. (Luke 15:27)

- The elder brother was self-important. He refused to leave the field unless his father entreated him to leave. (Luke 15:28)
- The elder brother was self-righteous. He extolled his own virtues and compared them to the lifestyle of his wasteful younger brother. (Luke 15:29)
- The elder brother was self-seeking. He coveted the attention given to his younger brother and wanted to have it all just for himself. (Luke 15:29-30)
- The elder brother was self-indulgent. Even though he was the firstborn and would inherit twice as much, he didn't want his father to share any of it with his needy younger brother. (Luke 15:31)

We are all like the prodigal son because our heavenly Father has forgiven our own sins and welcomed us back into his family. But if we should refuse to forgive others, then we will be more like the selfish elder brother, who was feeling unhappy, jealous, angry, resentful, depressed, and very miserable.

Perhaps you are wondering why even some who profess belief in Christianity still have unforgiveness in their hearts and become more like the selfish elder brother than the prodigal son. The reason is simply because we all have free will and we all are free to choose to do either good or evil.

This is also why we should submit our minds, wills, and emotions unto God and allow Him to transform us by the renewing of our minds so that we can know and do what is that "good, and acceptable, and perfect, will of God."

"I beseech you therefore, brethren, by the mercies of God, that ye present your bodies a living sacrifice, holy, acceptable unto God, which is your reasonable service. And be not conformed to this world: but be ye transformed by the renewing of your mind, that ye may prove what is that good, and acceptable, and perfect, will of God." (Romans 12:1-2)

Your soul and mine are still in the process of being "transformed by the renewing of our minds" to become more and more like Jesus. And this will not be completed until the day that you and I die and only what is like our Lord will be resurrected.

"But we all, with open face beholding as in a glass the glory of the Lord, are changed into the same image from glory to glory, even as by the Spirit of the Lord." (2 Corinthians 3:18)

Until then, the more we become like Jesus; the more we will be willing to love and forgive even those who have committed the worst of offenses against us.

"Blessed are the peacemakers: for they shall be called the children of God." (Matthew 5:9)

For us, we are always to love and forgive everyone and never condemn or judge anyone. But God can still override our own forgiveness and judge or condemn, for He is the only one who knows the thoughts and the intents of our hearts. So, our forgiveness of others may not always prevent God's wrath, but our prayers and intercession certainly can.

Prayer can mitigate or lessen God's judgment, as it did when Jesus prayed and interceded for us. As long as there is true repentance, we should always forgive. And even if there is no repentance, we should still pray and do whatever we can to help that person to repent of his or her bad behavior.

"Then came Peter to Him, and said, Lord, how oft shall my brother sin against me, and I forgive him? Till seven times? Jesus saith unto him, I say not unto thee, until seven times: but, until seventy times seven." (Matthew 18:21-22)

The words "seventy times seven" was the Lord's way of saying that we should always forgive. So if you are finding it difficult to forgive, I want you to know that God loves you and wants to set you free from the sin of unforgiveness so that you can live the abundant life that God desires for all of his children.

However, if you should accept the grace and the love of God and then refuse to extend to others the same forgiveness that you received, then your own lack of love and your unforgiveness could turn into a "root of bitterness and cause you to "fail of the grace of God."

"Follow peace with all men, and holiness, without which no man shall see the Lord: Looking diligently lest any man fail of the grace of God; lest any root of bitterness springing up trouble you, and thereby many be defiled" (Hebrews 12: 14-15)

I cannot emphasize strongly enough the importance of heeding our Lord's very stern warning that unforgiveness can have extreme and very drastic consequences both now and throughout all eternity.

"Be not deceived; God is not mocked: for whatsoever a man soweth, that shall he also reap." (Galatians 6:7)

So, if you are still holding on to unforgiveness, I pray that the following words will either scare you into at least making an attempt to forgive, or better yet get you to seek God for His help. And hopefully He will make you more than willing to forgive from your heart all who may have offended or caused you harm.

"Behold therefore the goodness and severity of God: on them which fell, severity; but toward thee, goodness, if thou continue in his goodness: otherwise thou also shalt be cut off." (Romans 11:22)

In what we call "the Lord's Prayer," Jesus taught us that we should pray for His heavenly Father to "forgive us our debts as we forgive our debtors." But then at the end of this suggested prayer, Jesus added the warning that if we should refuse to forgive others as we would like to be forgiven, then "neither will your Father forgive your trespasses!"

It is ironic that whenever the Lord's Prayer is publicly recited, virtually everyone will stop at the inserted word "amen." This leaves out a very significant part of the sermon where Jesus gave a very stern warning that our heavenly Father will not forgive our trespasses if we do not also forgive the trespasses of others.

"After this manner therefore pray ye: Our Father which art in heaven, Hallowed be thy name. Thy kingdom come, Thy will be done, on earth, as it is in heaven. Give us this day our daily bread. And forgive us our debts, as we forgive our debtors. And lead us not into temptation, but deliver us from evil: For Thine is the kingdom, and the power, and the glory, forever. Amen. For if ye forgive men their trespasses, your heavenly Father will also forgive you: But if ye forgive not men their trespasses, neither will your Father forgive your trespasses." (Matthew 6:9-15)

When Peter asked how many times he had to forgive, Jesus answered this question with a parable about an unforgiving servant who pleaded for mercy for himself and then refused to do the same for his fellow servant. (See Matthew 18:21-35)

In this parable, Jesus said that the kingdom of heaven was like the servant who pleaded with his king for forgiveness of a very large debt. Since the servant was unable to pay, the king had compassion on him and forgave him his entire debt.

But then afterwards, that same servant refused to forgive a fellow servant who was also unable to pay a very small debt and he even had the servant put into a debtor's prison. When the king found out about this, he was very angry and immediately put the unforgiving servant into the same debtor's prison. There he was turned over to the "torturers" until his previously forgiven debt was completely paid in full.

"Then his lord, after that he had called him, said unto him, O thou wicked servant, I forgave thee all that debt, because thou desiredst me: Shouldest not thou also have had compassion on thy fellow servant, even as I had pity on thee? And his lord was wroth, and delivered him to the tormentors, till he should pay all that was due unto him." (Matthew 18:32-34)

Jesus then concluded this parable with the very serious and specific warning that "So likewise shall my heavenly Father do also unto you, if ye from your hearts forgive not everyone his brother their trespasses." (Matthew 18:35)

Again, Jesus gave essentially the same warning about unforgiveness right after He preached His "mountain moving faith" sermon. He added the stern warning that "if ye do not forgive, neither will your Father which is in heaven forgive your trespasses."

"And when ye stand praying, forgive, if ye have ought against any: that your Father also which is in heaven may forgive you your trespasses. But if ye do not forgive, neither will your Father which is in heaven forgive your trespasses." (Mark 11:25-26)

So if you are still holding on to unforgiveness and wondering why your prayers are not being answered, then this is your answer. If you want to have your sins forgiven and your prayers answered, then you should make sure that you have forgiven everyone who may have offended or hurt you in any way.

If you are still having difficulty in forgiving someone, then you should ask for His help and humbly submit yourself to the will of God and earnestly pray the perfect prayer, which is: "Thy will be done in earth, as it is in heaven." (Matthew 6:10)

Then you should ask God for His grace and for His wisdom to know how to honestly and sincerely forgive that person from your heart. And if you ask in faith and do not doubt, He has already said that "it will be given to you."

"If any of you lacks wisdom, you should ask God, who gives generously to all without finding fault, and it will be given to you. But when you ask, you must believe and not doubt, because the one who doubts is like a wave of the sea, blown and tossed by the wind." (James 1:5-6 NIV)

Although this may not come right away, your forgiveness should eventually include even loving and praying for the person. Only then will you know for sure your own prayers will be answered and that you have avoided the just but severe consequences of unjustly holding on to unforgiveness.

Now is a good time to get free.

Perhaps now would be a good time for you to search your own heart and see if there is anyone else whom you have not yet forgiven. If someone comes to mind and you feel any anger, bitterness, or stiffness in your face when you think or talk about that person, then you will know that you have not really forgiven.

Who you have forgiven is really only between you and God, so you are not obligated to tell anyone the intimate details of your struggles unless you are prompted by the Holy Spirit or your own conscience.

If you really want to be completely free, then you should become as "transparent" as possible and openly confess your sins to others so that they can also pray with you that you may be healed. However, there are always some who are very prone to gossip so you should be careful whom you select to pray.

"Therefore confess your sins to each other and pray for each other so that you may be healed. The prayer of a righteous person is powerful and effective." (James 5:16 NIV)

When you openly admit and confess your feelings to others and ask for their prayers, this also liberates you from trying to hide your weaknesses or from worrying about someone finding out about them.

## God's Goodness, God's Justice

Billy Graham and countless others have often preached from John 3:16 the wonderful message of God's love, forgiveness, and our redemption:

For God so loved the world that He gave His only begotten Son, that whosoever believeth in Him should not perish, but have everlasting life." (John 3:16)

Most Christians and non-Christians alike like this verse and often repeat it because it reveals that our salvation is based upon our faith in what His only begotten Son has done and not upon our own futile efforts to become or look righteous on our own.

The following is a portion of the scrip-ture verses that immediately precede the verse in John 3: 16 which confirms and further clarifies that Jesus "came down from heaven" and why only those who believe in Him would have eternal life.

"And no man hath ascended up to heaven, but He that came down from heaven, even the Son of Man which is in heaven. And as Moses lifted up the serpent in the wilderness, even so must the Son of man be lifted up: That whosoever believeth in Him should not perish, but have eternal life." (John 3:13-15)

However, there is another side of our very righteous God that should also be revealed to all, but especially to unbelievers. The warning is based upon the fact that God's perfect love must also be kept in balance by his perfect justice.

Our Creator is still the personification of all that is good in love and in mercy, but He is a very holy and righteous God, so He must also be perfect in justice. That is also why His perfect justice had demanded the supreme sacrifice of His only begotten Son before He could justify His own forgiveness of all of          our sins.

In other verses that precede John 3:16 in the same chapter, Jesus first explained to Nicodemus, a ruler of the Jews, why we all must first be spiritually cleansed by being "born again" or "born from above" before we can even "see" or "enter" into the perfect eternal Kingdom of God.

And in the verses that immediately follow John 3:16, as quoted below, Jesus explained further why those who do not believe in the supreme sacrifice of the only begotten Son of God are condemned already, and why they will not be able to see or enter into the Kingdom of God if they do not repent.

"For God sent not His Son into the world to condemn the world; but that the world through Him might be saved. He that believeth on Him is not condemned: but He that believeth not is condemned already, because He hath not believed in the name of the only begotten Son of God. And this is the condemnation, that light is come into the world, and men loved darkness rather than light, because their deeds were evil. For everyone that doeth evil hateth the light, neither cometh to the light, lest his deeds should be reproved. But he that doeth truth cometh to the light, that his deeds may be made manifest, that they are wrought in God." (John 3:17-21)

And at the end of this same chapter, John the Baptist also confirmed that the "wrath of God" would remain upon all who refused to believe in the supreme sacrifice of the only begotten Son of God.

In other words, those who refuse to believe do not really want to know the truth because their deeds are evil, and they do not want to change. That is also why they refuse to believe even when their very own conscience reveals this to be true.

"Now the Spirit speaketh expressly, that in the latter times some shall depart from the faith, giving heed to seducing spirits, and doctrines of devils; Speaking lies in hypocrisy; having their conscience seared with a hot iron."   (I Timothy 4:1-2)

But once a person realizes that it is really true that "the wrath of God" must remain upon all unbelievers then it should be a very easy and a very logical decision to become a believer and thus avoid the punishment that comes to all who reject the love of God and the sacrifice of His only begotten Son.

"He that hath received His testimony hath set to his seal that God is true. For He whom God hath sent speaketh the words of God: for God giveth not the Spirit by measure unto him. The Father loveth the Son, and hath given all things into His hand. He that believeth on the Son hath everlasting life: and he that believeth not the Son shall not see life; but the wrath of God abideth on him."   (John 3:33-36)

We all have been given free will, so what we choose to believe and what we do will ultimately determine our own destiny. If you haven't done this already, I hope and pray that you will quickly repent and confess any unforgiveness or bitterness that you might still have and receive God's immediate forgiveness and cleansing. (1 John 1 :9)

And, of course, if you have never repented of your sins and been spiritually reborn by receiving Jesus (the promised Jewish Messiah) as your own personal Lord and Savior, then this would also be a good time to do this as well. Then you will be better able to understand the rest of this book.

"The word is nigh thee, even in thy mouth, and in thy heart: that is, the word of faith, which we preach; That if thou shalt confess with thy mouth the Lord Jesus, and shalt believe in thine heart that God hath raised Him from the dead, thou shalt be saved. For with the heart man believeth unto righteousness; and with the mouth confession is made unto salvation." (Romans 10:8-10)

I suspect that there will be some unbelievers and doubters reading this book who will strongly object to the fact that I have said that those who refuse to believe that salvation is only through the atoning sacrifice of His Son will have to endure the wrath of God and His righteous judgment.

"For therein is the righteousness of God revealed from faith to faith: as it is written, The just shall live by faith. For the wrath of God is revealed from heaven against all ungodliness and unrighteousness of men, who hold the truth in unrighteousness; Because that which may be known of God is manifest in them; for God hath shewed it unto them. For the invisible things of Him from the creation of the world are clearly seen, being understood by the things that are made, even His eternal power and Godhead; so that they are without excuse" (Romans 1:17-20)

However, in their defense, their unbelief and willful behavior may be at least partially because they do not fully understand the depths of their own depravity. And they do not fully understand the enormity of the sacrificial gift that has been offered to them by a God who really does love them. He only wants their souls to be saved from His perfect justice which requires that all unbelievers must suffer punishment.

"As surely as I live, declares the Sovereign Lord, I take no pleasure in the death of the wicked, but rather that they turn from their ways and live. Turn! Turn from your evil ways! Why will you die, people of Israel?" (Ezekiel 33:11 NIV)

The love of Jesus and His extreme sacrifice to save us are so enormous in the eyes of God that any rejection of His own beloved Son is an enormous "insult" to His Spirit of Grace. That is why His perfect justice can only respond to unbelievers with His righteous wrath and their ultimate rejection from His perfect heaven.

"Anyone who rejected the Law of Moses died without mercy on the testimony of two or three witnesses. How much more severely do you think someone deserves to be punished who has trampled the Son of God underfoot, who has treated as an unholy thing the blood of the covenant that sanctified them, and who has insulted the Spirit of grace?" (Hebrews 10:28-29 NIV)

If we could fully comprehend just how much and how intensely our heavenly Father loves His only begotten Son Jesus Christ and His Holy Spirit, then we might be more appreciative of the enormity of their sacrificial gifts that have been given to us.

And the intense love of God the Father, the Son, and the Holy Spirit for each other is so great that the Father would not release the fullness of his precious Holy Spirit to us until His precious Son first returned to Heaven to be with Him.

"Nevertheless, I tell you the truth; It is expedient for you that I go away: for if I go not away, the Comforter will not come unto you; but if I depart, I will send Him unto you. And when He is come, He will reprove the world of sin, and of righteousness, and of judgment." (John 16:7-8)

When this age of grace eventually does end and Jesus returns with His saints to rule and reign on the earth, the fullness of the Holy Spirit must return to God the Father and the people on earth will then be ruled directly by Jesus Christ and His resurrected saints for about one thousand years. (Revelation 14:1-5, 20:4)

"For we must all appear before the judgment seat of Christ; that every one may receive the things done in His body, according to that He hath done, whether it be good or bad." (2 Corinthians 5:10)

There are two judgment days men-tioned in the Bible. The first one will be by Jesus Christ when He returns to rule on earth for one thousand years. The second one will be by the Father and will be the final judgment of all mankind. (Revelation 20: 1 1-15) Only then will there be a New Heaven and a New Earth.

"And I heard a great voice out of heaven saying, Behold, the tabernacle of God is with men, and He will dwell with them, and they shall be His people, and God Himself shall be with them, and be their God. And God shall wipe away all tears from their eyes; and there shall be no more death, neither sorrow, nor crying, neither shall there be any more pain: for the former things are passed away." (Revelation 21:3-4)

The new earth will be similar to our present earth. We will all have beautiful new "personalized" homes to live in, and everyone will have things to do that will be similar to what we have learned on earth.

"In my Father's house are many mansions: if it were not so, I would have told you. I go to prepare a place for you. And if I go and prepare a place for you, I will come again, and receive you unto myself; that where I am, there ye may be also." (John 14:2-3)

## Hell and Anger

Many wonder how a loving God can justify creating a hell for those who reject His love and the love of His Son Jesus Christ.

Some even use this as an excuse not to believe, but the souls of angels and humans were both created to be eternal beings. And God cannot lie, so there has to be a place to put those who do not love Him, or Heaven would eventually be ruined.

"And beside all this, between us and you there is a great gulf fixed: so that they which would pass from hence to you cannot; neither can they pass to us, that would come from thence." (Luke 16:26)

Hell was originally "prepared for the devil and his angels" (Matthew 25:41) as sort of a dumping ground for the angels who had full knowledge and yet openly rebelled against God. But man was made in the image of God and tempted by Satan, so it was never God's perfect will that they should ever have to suffer the same fate.

"Have I any pleasure at all that the wicked should die? saith the Lord God: and not that he should return from his ways, and live?" (Ezekiel 18:23)

Even those righteous believers who lived and died before Jesus came could not go to Heaven without Jesus but they were still kept safely in a higher part of hell called "Abraham's bosom" until Jesus died on the cross and "preached unto the spirits in prison."

"For Christ also hath once suffered for sins, the just for the unjust, that He might bring us to God, being put to death in the flesh, but quickened by the Spirit: By which also He went and preached unto the spirits in prison; Which sometime were disobedient, when once the longsuffering of God waited in the days of Noah, while the ark was a preparing, wherein few, that is, eight souls were saved by water." (1 Peter 3:18-20)

Hell is truly a terrible place, but no human being has to ever go there no matter what they have done. All they have to do is repent of their obvious sins and believe what our Lord Jesus Christ has done for them, and they will be saved from it.

After His resurrection, Jesus told His disciples that now "repentance and the remission of sins should be preached in his name among all nations, beginning at Jerusalem." This means that all peoples, both Jews and Gentiles, can now repent and believe in the supreme sacrifice of Jesus for the remission of their sins and they can all go to Heaven when they die.

"And said unto them, Thus it is written, and thus it behooved Christ to suffer, and to rise from the dead the third day: And that repentance and remission of sins should be preached in His name among all nations, beginning at Jerusalem." (Luke 24:46-47)

The Greek word (aphesis) used here for the word "remission" means to forgive, pardon, or to permanently release a person from bondage or imprisonment. In other words, when we forgive someone or when we are forgiven by God, it should be just as if the sins had never even happened!

Keep yourself from anger. In order to justify themselves, unbelievers usually re-spond with an elaborate intellectual array of human self-effort and self-righteousness to save themselves, along with very illogical and obtuse human reasoning as to why they do not really have to repent of their decadent lifestyle or why they have to believe anything that was written so long ago in the Bible.

When people do not believe the Bible or that they should love God and forgive even their enemies, they will often get very angry. But you will not be able to help them if you also get angry in return, so don't forget that a "soft answer" is what will turn away their anger so that they can receive the truth.

"A soft answer turneth away wrath: but grievous words stir up anger. The tongue of the wise useth knowledge aright: but the mouth of fools poureth out foolishness." (Proverbs 15:1-2)

And almost everyone will express at least some anger whenever they see or ex-perience gross injustice, or if circumstances become just too hard to bear. But if you are already walking closely with the Lord, you will be more like the Lord and be "slow to anger" and "abounding in love." And you will also partake of His many other attributes and be quick to love and forgive even those who may have caused you harm.

"The Lord is compassionate and gracious; slow to anger, abounding in love. He will not always accuse, nor will he harbor his anger forever; he does not treat us as our sins deserve or repay us according to our iniquities. For as high as the heavens are above the earth, so great is his love for those who fear him." (Psalm 103: 8-11 NIV)

Your first line of defense against having anger is to pray and spend quality time with the

Lord and either avoid or have no close friendships with whoever is constantly angry or negative. For if you have close relationships with those who are frequently angry, you will soon find yourself becoming just like them.

"Make no friendship with an angry man; and with a furious man thou shalt not go: Lest thou learn his ways, and get a snare to thy soul." (Proverbs 22:2425)

If you are already connected closely by marriage, employment, or by any other ways to those who are continuously angry, then it is even more important for you to know how to still love and forgive them. Even when you are in the company of those who are constantly angry and stirring up strife, you can learn how to cope and still remain free from anger.

"An angry man stirreth up strife, and a furious man aboundeth in transgression." (Proverbs 29:22)

A "railer" is someone who bitterly and continuously complains about a person or situation. And the Bible says that a little leaven can spoil the whole lump, so the apostle Paul went even further.

After wisely adding the disclaimer that it is not possible to avoid all "fornicators of this world, or with the covetous, or extortioners, or with idolaters," he advised us all to avoid as much as possible close relationships with such people and not to even eat with them.

"I wrote unto you in an epistle not to company with fornicators: Yet not altogether with the fornicators of this world, or with the covetous, or extortioners, or with idolaters; for then must ye needs go out of the world. But now I have written unto you not to keep company, if any man that is called a brother be a fornicator, or covetous, or an idolator, or a railer, or a drunkard, or an extortioner; with such an one no not to eat." (1 Corinthians 5:9-11)

At first being angry is not a sin as long as there is a just cause, and you may think that this applies to your own situation. But even if you think you can justify your anger, it will still become a sin if you should keep it for more than one day. (Ephesians 4:26)

## Anger becomes Depression

Anger and depression can come from any number of sources such as from the loss or a job, a home, finances, or of a loved one. Anger can also come from personal  trauma, or rejection from fellow workers, friends, or even family.

Depression has sometimes been described as being "anger turned inward", but there are also other causes so if you should happen to feel depressed, this does not necessarily mean that you also have either suppressed anger or a root of bitterness.

The feelings of intense anger or despair will almost always accompany all kinds of negative emotions. So if you are still holding on to any negative emotions in your heart for any reason whatsoever, then you will also be most likely very susceptible to having cycles of depression or angry outbursts of anger.

But you can know for sure that you are holding on to unforgiveness or a root of bitterness if intense angry feelings should rise up whenever you think about or talk about a particular person or situation. If you do not repent of this and forgive, then this condition will continue until you eventually either forgive or find and resolve the root cause of your anger.

Whenever anger is suppressed without first being resolved, it can easily turn into depression and bring spiritual death to your soul. In its early stages, you may switch back and forth from angry outbursts to passive depression; and then from passive depression to angry outbursts.

While the anger is openly expressed, you will no longer feel depressed. But when the anger is again suppressed, the depression will gradually return.

The anger and depression cycle is very similar to the cycles of manic depression or bipolar disorders as they also have wide mood swings. The root cause of these disorders are also often anger, so the venting of the anger will also not provide a permanent cure and the suppression of the anger will only eventually lead back into depression.

This cycle can be expected to continue back and forth until the root cause is ultimately discovered and resolved. If this should not be resolved within a reasonable length of time, the person could even lose hope and develop serious psychotic symptoms.

And the person could even become suicidal or lapse into a permanent state of clinical depression or even become catatonic. For those who have gone through a traumatic event like a war, an assault, or a disaster, they may want to contact the government sponsored National Center for Posttraumatic Stress Disorder.

In these much more severe cases, highly trained professional care with additional medical or nutritional treatment may be necessary, so these cases would obviously be beyond the scope of this book.

But if the person does not have a severe clinical or psychotic condition, then he or she may only need to attend anger management classes or some form of group therapy; or maybe receive private counseling from a church pastor or a trained Christian counselor.

And even better yet, if you are the one who has been frequently angry or depressed and you can now see that this may be because of your own selfishness and a lack of forgiveness or love and compassion for others, then you have taken a giant step towards your own complete recovery.

## Hope becomes Faith

There is always hope in God.

"Hope deferred makes the heart sick, but a longing fulfilled is a tree of life." (Proverbs 13:12 NIV)

Maybe you are feeling angry right now; or maybe your anger has been suppressed and you have fallen into a state of depression. It does not matter which state you are in; what is most important right now is that your hope in God must first be restored, for He is your ultimate source of all good things.

You cannot do anything about what has happened to you in the past, but you can always have hope in the "God of hope" for He is always able to change things for the better and He can even fill you with positive feelings of "joy and peace" while He is doing this.

"May the God of hope fill you with all joy and peace as you trust in Him, so that you may overflow with hope by the power of the Holy Spirit. " (Romans 15:13 NIV)

When my mother-in-law's husband died, she admitted that she was very angry with him "for having left her here alone." She knew that he did not die on purpose, but she was still very angry. She was afraid to blame God, so she became very depressed when she realized she couldn't do anything about it.

Well, she was easily cured when she remarried. It is normal for anyone to miss a loved one who has died, but the apostle Paul advised us to "sorrow not, even as others which have no hope." For if you believe in Jesus and that He died and rose again, then you will see your loved ones again who also believed in Jesus.

"But I would not have you to be ignorant, brethren, concerning them which are asleep, that ye sorrow not, even as others which have no hope. For if we believe that Jesus died and rose again, even so them also which sleep in Jesus will God bring with Him. (I Thessalonians 4:13-14)

Sometimes it is necessary to release your emotional feelings with weeping, and especially when a loved one dies or when you are overwhelmed with adverse circumstances. But if you have hope in God, you may weep, but you will have joy in the morning.

"Weeping may endure for a night, but joy cometh in the morning." (Psalm 30:5)

Weeping is like an emotional safety valve. When the emotional pressure becomes too great, the valve opens up and tears are released. Of course, I am not encouraging anyone to weep out of weakness or self-pity, for Jesus never wept even when He was being criticized, beaten, or crucified.

And when Jesus wept over the city of Jerusalem it was because He knew that the people were about to experience the just judgment of God for their rejection of Him and His ministry. His weeping was therefore because of His love and compassion for them and was obviously not because He had lost hope.

"And when He was come near, He beheld the city, and wept over it, Saying, If thou hadst known, even thou, at least in this thy day, the things which belong unto thy peace! But now they are hid from thine eyes." (Luke 19: 41-42)

Even the most righteous saints of God like Job, King David, and the prophets Elijah and Jeremiah (who was even called "the weeping prophet") and many others in the Bible have at times had to release their emotions with weeping.

When King David became weary from constantly being under attack by his enemies, he said, "I water my couch with my tears. Mine eye is consumed because of grief."

"I am weary with my groaning; all the night make I my bed to swim; I water my couch with my tears. Mine eye is consumed because of grief; it waxeth old because of all mine enemies. Depart from me, all ye workers of iniquity; for the Lord hath heard the voice of my weeping. The Lord hath heard my supplication; the Lord will receive my prayer." (Psalm 6:6-9)

The writer of the forty-second psalm also suffered from feelings of hopelessness and depression, but this changed after he went into the church and prayed. He was able to encourage himself by "speaking" to his soul to have hope in God. He was then able to praise God ahead of time for his help with the following exhortation that he repeated three times for emphasis.

"Why art thou cast down, oh my soul? And why art thou disquieted in me? Hope thou in God, for I shall yet praise him for the help of His countenance." (Psalm 42:5)

The cure for depression and hope-lessness begins with our hope and trust in our loving and almighty God and is completed when it turns into faith in His ability to change our lives for the better.

"For we are saved by hope: but hope that is seen is not hope: for what a man seeth, why doth he yet hope for? But if we hope for that we see not, then do we with patience wait for it. Likewise, the Spirit also helpeth our infirmities: for we know not what we should pray for as we ought: but the Spirit itself maketh intercession for us with groanings which cannot be uttered." (Romans 8:24-26)

Hope is an expectancy that good will ultimately triumph, and the basis for our hope is in the manifestation of God's love and compassion. And when you realize His awe-some power and the amount of love that God has for you and all of his children, then hope can give birth to faith.

Faith works by love so when you truly love God and believe that He loves you, then it should be easy to have faith that He will help you to forgive whoever has offended you and to be delivered from all anger.

"For we through the Spirit wait for the hope of righteousness by faith. For in Jesus Christ neither circumcision availeth any thing, nor uncircumcision; but faith which worketh by love." (Galatians 5:5-6)

Faith simply believes what God says to be true. I used to think that the Greek words for "faith" (pistis) and "believe" (pisteuo) were different words, but they both have the same meaning except that one happens to be a noun and one a verb.

Faith initially comes by either reading or hearing the preaching of the "general" (logos) Word of God. The believing in our hearts comes when the Holy Spirit in us confirms that the "specific" (rhema) Word of God that we received is absolutely true.

"As it is written, How beautiful are the feet of them that preach the gospel of peace, and bring glad tidings of good things! But they have not all obeyed the gospel. For Esaias [Isaiah] saith, Lord, who hath believed our report? So then faith cometh by hearing, and hearing by the word [rhema] of God. (Romans 10:15-17)

The writings of James gave a proper balance to Paul's writings on faith and works. Both are true and both were apostles, but the writings of Paul were focused more on the eternal doctrinal teachings, for he was also an "evangelist." And the writings of James were focused more on meeting the physical needs of his congregation, for he was also the "pastor" of the Church in Jerusalem.

"What good is it, my brothers and sisters, if someone claims to have faith but has no deeds? Can such faith save them? Suppose a brother or a sister is without clothes and daily food. If one of you says to them, "Go in peace; keep warm and well fed, but does nothing about their physical needs, what good is it? In the same way, faith by itself, if it is not accompanied by action, is dead. But someone will say, 'You have faith; I have deeds.' Show me your faith without deeds, and I will show you my faith by my deeds." (James 2:14-18 NIV)

God may use a book, a friend, a church pastor, a trained counselor, or even a nutritionist or a medical doctor, to help set you free. But your hope and your faith should always remain in almighty God, for He is the ultimate source of all good things.

And even if you should still have some doubts, you can always pray like the father who wanted to believe for the healing of his young son, so he said to Jesus, "Lord, I believe, help thou mine unbelief."

"Jesus said unto him, If thou canst believe, all things are possible to Him that believeth. And straightway the father of the child cried out, and said with tears, Lord, I believe, help thou mine unbelief!" (Mark 9: 23-24)

Once you pray and establish your hope in the love and the goodness of God and your faith in His ability to help you, then this will immediately break the curse of depression. Whenever genuine faith comes in, depression will always leave, for "faith is the substance of things hoped for, the evidence of things not seen." (Hebrews 11: 1)

"Cast not away therefore your confidence, which hath great recompence of reward. For ye have need of patience, that, after ye have done the will of God, ye might receive the promise. For yet a little while, and he that shall come will come, and will not tarry. Now the just shall live by faith: but if any man draw back, my soul shall have no pleasure in him. But we are not of them who draw back unto perdition; but of them that believe to the saving of the soul." (Hebrews 10:12-39)

Nevertheless, in order to receive anything by faith, you must not only believe the Word of God, but you must do what you say that you believe and not doubt. And it is also very important that you speak out what you believe by faith to be true. You cannot always control what you are thinking, but you can always control what you are speaking.

"And Jesus answering saith unto them, Have faith in God. For verily I say unto you, That whosoever shall say unto this mountain, Be thou removed, and be thou cast into the sea; and shall not doubt in his heart, but shall believe that those things which he saith shall come to pass; he shall have whatsoever he saith.' Therefore I say unto you, What things so ever ye desire, when ye pray, believe that ye receive them, and ye shall have them." (Mark 11:22-24)

And once you have established your faith in almighty God by speaking and believing His

Word, then you are emotionally free to take the next step, which is to deal with any anger which might have caused you to feel depressed or bitter.

## Anger with a Cause

If you are angry and "without a cause", then your anger cannot be justified. It is perfectly normal to be angry over injustice, but your anger must still be justified and not prolonged. So if you have not repented, then you could be bringing upon yourself the righteous judgment of God.

In the following scripture, there were three examples given by Jesus of unjust anger and its consequences. They were already written in the Law of Moses to correct those who were angry "without a cause" and to encourage them to repent.

"Ye have heard that it was said of them of old time, Thou shalt not kill; and whosoever shall kill shall be in danger of the judgment: But I say unto you, That whosoever is angry with his brother without a cause shall be in danger of the judgment: and whosoever shall say to his brother, 'Raca!', [an Aramaic term of contempt] shall be in danger of the council: but whosoever shall say, 'Thou fool', shall be in danger of hellfire." (Matthew 5:21-22)

- Jesus first made the danger of the judgment for unjust anger the same as the judgment that was already in the Law of Moses for killing a person.
- If the unjust anger was also linked with contempt and disrespect for a Jewish brother, then the judgment of God was even greater. And under the law, the person could be brought before the council for disciplinary action and corrective punishment.
- If the angry person was so arrogant and unkind as to deliberately humiliate his Jewish brother in front of others by calling him a "fool," then he was in even greater danger for he could be cast into the worst part of hell when he died.

All of these judgments were given while they were still under the strict Law of Moses, and we are now under a new a much better covenant of Grace where the punishment for our sins have already been paid by the sacrifice of Jesus Christ. However, the Mosaic Laws can still be helpful in revealing the severity and the harm that our unjust anger can cause.

Under our New Covenant of Grace, we should now continue to love and forgive even our enemies and "not be overcome by evil but overcome evil with good" for even our enemies could now repent of their sins and become spiritually reborn Christians.

And if any correction is required, we should never seek retaliation or revenge, for our Creator is the only one who can properly and fairly execute judgment, for He is the only one who knows the thoughts and the intents of our hearts. (Hebrews 4: 12)

"Do not take revenge, my dear friends, but leave room for God's wrath, for it is written: "It is mine to avenge; I will repay", says the Lord. On the contrary: "If your enemy is hungry, feed him; if he is thirsty, give him something to drink. In doing this, you will heap burning coals on his head." Do not be overcome by evil, but overcome evil with good." (Romans 12:19-21 NIV)

It is also very important to avoid making any major decisions while you are still angry. Only after you have your anger under control should you even try to search your own heart to see if your anger was really justified or not.

Before you take any action to correct any injustice done to you or to others, you should first humble yourself and pray for God's help. You should then be able to get your anger under control by "casting all your cares upon him, for he cares for you." It may also be helpful to take an "emotional time out" and get alone for a while with God so that you can more easily seek and receive His help and direction.

"Humble yourselves therefore under the mighty hand of God, that He may exalt you in due time: Casting all your care upon Him; for He careth for you." (1 Peter 5:6-7)

We all have a tendency in our carnal nature to want to "get even" whenever in-justice has been done to ourselves, but when the same thing is done to others, we are often very tolerant and forgiving.

This is, of course, hypocritical and our self-righteous anger is then often excused as being "righteous anger" when it is really either "unjust anger, wrath, or rage."

*Wrath* is anger with the intention of taking vengeance upon those causing the injustice.

"Wherefore, my beloved brethren, let every man be swift to hear, slow to speak, slow to wrath: For the wrath of man worketh not the righteousness of God." (James 1:19-20)

*Rage* is violent anger that is completely out of control and can never be justified.

"Who by the mouth of thy servant David hast said, Why did the heathen rage, and the people imagine vain things?" (Acts 4:25)

Prior events can also be the root cause of our anger. When people receive counseling, they often discover that traumatic experiences which happened in the past were really the root cause of their anger.

I once read in a newspaper of a young woman who had severely beaten up a burglar. She later admitted that she had just broken up with her boyfriend, and she had taken all her anger out on the burglar.

When the Police finally arrived, the burglar was very grateful. I am sure that the young woman felt much better, but I cannot say the same for the burglar!

You may also discover that the reason you have been overreacting in anger is because of some past experiences. If you think this might be your situation, you should ask God for His help and then honestly search your heart to see if any of these things have been hidden in your subconscious:

- If your anger is justified and under control, then you should pray and take appropriate action to help correct whatever caused it.
- If your anger has been prolonged or cannot be justified, then you should quickly confess this to God just as you would any other sin so you   can receive his forgiveness and be cleansed from all unrighteousness. (1 John 1 :9)
- If your anger was caused by severe trauma or is accompanied by symptoms such as panic attacks, phobias, etc. then you should also confess this to God, but you may also need additional counseling by others as well.

Jesus gives us an example of *justified anger*.

It may comfort you to know that Jesus was angry at times, but His anger was always justified while ours is not. And He did not sin for His anger was righteous as it was over of the injustice being done to others and it was not prolonged for more than one day.

Jesus became angry when He saw how cold and indifferent the Pharisees were to the needs of the man who had been suffering for a long time from a paralyzed hand. The Pharisees had coldly and legalistically decided that Jesus should not heal him because the Mosaic Law did not allow any "work" to be done on the Sabbath (Saturday).

Mark 3:5 "And when He [Jesus] had looked round about on them with anger, being grieved for the hardness of their hearts, He saith unto the man, 'Stretch forth thine hand. And he stretched it out; and his hand was restored as whole as the other."

Even though Jesus was angry, He did not allow his anger to continue into the next day. We know this because He immediately released it by first rebuking them for the hardness of their hearts and then by taking immediate action to correct the injustice by healing the man. He also corrected them by teaching that the man's healing was far more important than their legalistic observation of the Sabbath.

It is also reasonable to assume that Jesus was at least a little angry when He saw the greedy money changers in the temple cheating the faithful worshipers of God and making the sacred house of God "a den of thieves." He had been in the Temple the day before, but He did not act upon that anger until His Heavenly Father directed him to do so.

"And Jesus went into the temple of God and cast out all them that sold and bought in the temple, and overthrew the tables of the money-changers, and the seats of them that sold doves, and said unto them, It is written, My house shall be called the house of prayer, but ye have made it a den of thieves!" (Matthew 21: 12-13)

Jesus is our perfect example of how we should all live. In both cases, Jesus was angry over the injustice done to others, but He was never angry whenever the injustice was done to Himself.

"Christ also suffered for us, leaving us an example, that ye should follow His steps; who did no sin, neither was guile found in His mouth; who when He was reviled, reviled not again; when He suffered, He threatened not, but committed Himself to Him [God] who judgeth righteously." (1 Peter 2:20-23)

Whenever He was treated unfairly, He would just commit it unto His heavenly Father who knows the 'thoughts and intents" of all of our hearts (Hebrews 4: 12) and will always judge righteously.

And we should also do the same.

## Freedom from Anger

Even if you think you have a very good reason to be angry, it will still become a sin and an opportunity for the enemy to torment you if you should hold on to your anger for longer than one day.

Anger is a lot like fresh fruit or fresh vegetables. At first anger can be good for you by motivating you to correct some injustice or problem, but then if you should keep it too long, it will "spoil" and turn into "wrath" which usually also includes a strong desire for getting revenge.

"Be ye angry, and sin not; let not the sun go down upon your wrath; neither give place to the devil." (Ephesians 4:26-27)

No matter how much injustice you may have suffered (or how much you think you have suffered) you can still be free from all anger even before the day is over. Now you are probably thinking: "How it is even possible to gain control over such a strong emotion in only one day?"

The answer is surprisingly simple and very easy to do but you must be honest and sincere. Because of the victory that Jesus has already accomplished, you can be cleansed from the sin of unjustified or prolonged anger the same way that you are cleansed from any other sin. All you have to do is admit or confess to God that you are angry, and that you need his help to gain control over it.

You don't have to do anything else because you are now relying upon the goodness and the faithfulness of God and not upon your own efforts or ability to control your own anger. I have had to do this many times myself and it has always worked for me, so I believe this will also work for you and others as well.

"If we claim to have fellowship with Him and yet walk in the darkness, we lie and do not live out the truth. But if we walk in the light, as He is in the light, we have fellowship with one another, and the blood of Jesus, His Son, purifies us from all sin. If we claim to be without sin, we deceive ourselves and the truth is not in us. If we confess our sins, He is faithful and just and will forgive us our sins and purify us from all unrighteousness." (1 John 1:6-9 NIV)

The Greek word for confess is "homologia" which means to speak the same thing (as God) so as soon as you admit that you are angry and need His help to overcome it, the process of inner healing begins. Unless you have developed a deep seated "root of bitterness" you should find yourself free from all anger even before the day is over.

And once you have confessed and repented of any unjust anger, it should be much easier to forgive whoever or whatever your anger might have been directed against. If you have already done this, then you should now be in the process of being cleansed by a merciful God from all of your unrighteousness in accordance with the previous scripture.

Another very good reason for not holding on to anger, whether it is just or unjust anger, is that it can destroy your health. It is therefore very important that you become free from all anger as soon as possible.

Our physical bodies were designed by God so that our adrenal glands would activate; our hearts would beat faster; and our entire bodies would be energized whenever we are angry or fearful.

This is called the "fight or flight" response, and it was originally intended by God to provide instant energy and strength to cope with any danger or emergency situation. But if this state is prolonged, then the other bodily functions will be deprived of their normal energy and nutritional needs.

Prolonged anger and especially stress will therefore cause various organs of your body to slow down or malfunction. Prolonged anger will also suppress your immune system and cause you to become much more susceptible to various diseases.

Aggression and violence are obviously inappropriate forms of behavior for the release of the extra energy when you are angry. Until the root cause of your anger is discovered and resolved, a more appropriate response would be to release this energy with some form of appropriate physical activity.

If you are frequently angry over a variety of causes, and are having difficulty in controlling it, a regular exercise or sports program would probably be the best long-term solution. This will not only relieve your symptoms, but it will improve your overall health and physical fitness as well.

"Beloved, I wish above all things that thou mayest prosper and be in health, even as thy soul prospereth." (3 John 2)

## Acceptances

"Trust in the Lord with all thine heart; and lean not unto thine own understanding. In all thy ways acknowledge him, and He shall direct thy paths." (Proverbs 3: 5-6)

After you have gained control over your anger; forgiven and prayed for those who caused it; and then taken action to correct what can be changed, you should then be willing to accept your present situation as it is and not necessarily as you would have liked it to be.

Happiness and contentment does not come from always having your own way but rather from accepting the things that you cannot change. When the apostle Paul wrote about how he had learned to be content in every situation, he was still being persecuted and held unjustly in a prison in Rome.

"Not that I speak in respect of want: for I have learned, in whatsoever state I am, therewith to be content. I know both how to be abased, and I know how to abound: everywhere and in all things I am instructed both to be full and to be hungry, both to abound and to suffer need. I can do all things through Christ which strengtheneth me." (Philippians 4:11-13)

And Paul was still in the Roman prison when he wrote to the Philippians church that was supporting him with the often-quoted words that "my God shall supply all your need according to His riches in glory by Christ [Messiah] Jesus." (Philippians 4: 19)

Satan must have thought that he had a major victory when he inspired people to put Paul in prison, but if he was really smart, he would have inspired people to take away Paul's pen and parchment!

Of course, acceptance does not mean that you should not pray or do anything to change your situation to make it better. When the apostle Paul said, "I have learned, in whatsoever state I am, therewith to be content," I am sure that he would still have preferred to have been released from the prison.

Acceptance simply means that you should patiently accept your present situation without complaining or adopting a "victim" mentality and then do what Jesus did when He was unjustly reviled and treated badly. Jesus did not threaten anyone or revile back. He just committed it all to his heavenly Father whom He knew would always judge righteously.

"For what glory is it, if, when ye be buffeted for your faults, ye shall take it patiently? But if, when ye do well, and suffer for it, ye take it patiently, this is acceptable with God. For even hereunto were ye called: because Christ also suffered for us, leaving us an example, that ye should follow His steps: Who did no sin, neither was guile found in His mouth: Who, when He was reviled, reviled not again; when He suffered, He threatened not; but committed Himself to Him that judgeth righteously" (I Peter 2: 20-23)

Reinhold Niebuhr summed this all up very well in what we now call "the Serenity Prayer". This prayer has also been used very effectively in the rehabilitation of people in various self-help groups like Alcoholics Anonymous.

*"God, grant me the serenity to accept the things I cannot change;*

*The courage to change the things I can;*

*And the wisdom to know the difference."*

If you are still unable to forgive or be content with your present situation, then you may have developed a "root of bitterness."

This is a much more severe and complex condition than unforgiveness and the way to become free from it will be discussed later in part three of this book.

# Part II

---

# It's All About Love

*Jesus is the way to God's love.*

"Thomas said to him, 'Lord, we don 't know where you are going, so how can we show the way?' Jesus answered, 'I am the way and the truth and the life. No one comes to the Father except through me. If you really know me, you will know my father as well. From now on, you do know Him and have seen Him." (John 14: 5-7 NIV)

Jesus, who preexisted as the Word of God, loved us so much that He was willing to take in humanity and suffer and die on the cross as atonement for our sins. And as both the Son of God and the Son of Adam, Jesus is the only one who could take our punishment and thus fulfill the perfect justice of God.

"Then said Mary unto the angel, How shall this be, seeing I know not a man? And the angel answered and said unto her, The Holy Ghost shall come upon thee, and the power of the Highest shall overshadow thee: therefore also that holy thing which shall be born of thee shall be called the Son of God." (Luke 1:34-35)

And His resurrection from the dead was witnessed and confirmed by over 500 people (Acts 1:4-5) and later confirmed by the Holy Spirit of God on the day of Pentecost (Acts 2:1-2) as well as by an unknown number of miracles done in His name (Acts 4:14-17) which have continued to be manifested throughout the earth for almost two thousand years.

"Consequently, just as one trespass resulted in condemnation for all people, so also one righteous act resulted in justification and life for all people. For just as through the disobedience of the one man [Adam] the many were made sinners, so also through the obedience of the one man [Jesus] the many will be made righteous." (Romans 5:18-19 NIV)

The Bible very clearly states that there is only "one mediator between God and men, the man, Christ Jesus" (1 Timothy 2:5) and Jesus Himself openly declared to His disciples that "I am the way, the truth, and the life; no man cometh unto the Father except by me." (John 14:6) And there are many other Scriptures which also confirm the divinity of Christ. (John 8:58, Revelation 1:17-18, etc.)

The apostle Peter confirmed no church traditions or rituals can save our souls. This was confirmed when he said, "There is no other name under heaven given among men, whereby we must be saved." (Acts 4:12)

The apostle Paul made it very clear that even our own good works cannot save us from hell, for he said that it is only "by grace are you saved through faith; and that not of yourselves, it is a gift of God; not of works lest any man should boast." (Ephesians 2:9)

In addition, secular historians have recorded that Peter and the other disciples of Jesus were willing to be tortured and killed rather than deny their faith. And except for the apostle John, who lived a very long life in exile on the Isle of Patmos in Greece, all of the original disciples of Jesus died as martyrs.

How could they have possibly done this if they had any doubts? And if the disciples of Jesus were themselves deceivers, wouldn't you think that at least one of them would admit it in order to avoid almost certain torture and death? It seems to me to be a very logical conclusion that the Biblical account of Jesus and His death and resurrection must therefore be true.

And today there is so much more historical, empirical, archeological, and newly found evidence supporting the Bible that believing it to be true should be considered as the only logical conclusion even to the most intellectual of human minds.

There is far more historical evidence of the existence, beliefs, and the teachings of Jesus than there is of the Roman Emperor Julius Caesar. So to reject the truth recorded in the Bible without at least making a thorough study of the facts just does not even make any sense!

There were some clues from various prophets that God was going to put a new Spirit within us (Ezekiel 11:19) and pour out His Spirit upon all flesh (Joel 2:28) but even His disciples did not realize they were going to have the Spirit of Christ live in their hearts.

This mystery was kept hidden on purpose, for if Satan and the evil Princes of this world had known, "they would not have crucified the Lord of Glory." (1 Corinthians 2:8)

"Even the mystery which hath been hid from ages and from generations, but now is made manifest to His saints: To whom God would make known what is the riches of the glory of this mystery among the Gentiles; which is Christ in you, the hope of glory" (Colossians 1:26-27)

## Jesus is our Eternal High Priest

The love of Jesus for the lost caused Him to agree to become a man and take upon Himself our sins just so that He could suffer and die as atonement for the sins of all mankind and be our eternal High Priest and our mediator "between God and mankind."

"Wherefore, holy brethren, partakers of the heavenly calling, consider the Apostle and High Priest of our profession, Christ Jesus; Who was faithful to Him that appointed Him, as also Moses was faithful in all his house. For this man was counted worthy of more glory than Moses, inasmuch as he who hath builded the house hath more honor than the house." (Hebrews 3:1-3)

The Old Covenant Laws that God gave to Moses were necessary at that time to help restrain the evils of that generation. And they can still be helpful as they contain many principles, prophecies, and ordinances that promote morality, righteous behavior, excellent health, and prosperous living.

But now, because of the love and sacrifice of Jesus, we have a new and a much better covenant with our God. The previous covenant only promised temporary forgiveness of sins, but it never promised to grant the much greater blessings of eternal life and intimate communion and fellowship with our very holy Creator as "children of God by faith in Christ Jesus."

"Wherefore the law was our schoolmaster to bring us unto Christ, that we might be justified by faith. But after that faith is come, we are no longer under a school master, for ye are all the children of God by faith in Christ Jesus." (Galatians 3: 24-26)

The New Covenant is so much better for we are now "no longer under a schoolmaster" and are living by faith, for we have the love of Jesus continuously abiding in us. And even if we should sin, we know that He is now our High Priest and that "we have an Advocate with the Father, Jesus Christ the righteous."

"My little children, these things write I unto you, that ye sin not. And if any man sin, we have an advocate with the Father, Jesus Christ the righteous: And He is the propitiation for our sins: and not for ours only, but also for the sins of the whole world." (1 John 2:1-2)

Instead of obeying an enormous system of rules and regulations under the Old Covenant, we can now simply yield unto the gentle promptings of Christ within us. This is also what the apostle Paul believed, taught, and lived to the fullest as a true disciple of our Lord Jesus Christ.

"For I through the law am dead to the law, that I might live unto God. I am crucified with Christ: nevertheless I live; yet not I, but Christ liveth in me: and the life which I now live in the flesh I live by the faith of the Son of God, who loved me, and gave Himself for me. I do not frustrate the grace of God: for if righteousness come by the law, then Christ is dead in vain." (Galatians 2: 19-21)

- Before Jesus came, the blood of animals was used as a substitute under the Old Covenant to temporarily "cover" the sins of the people for only one year. Now the atoning blood of Jesus permanently pardons and "removes" our sins!
- Before Jesus came, only the High Priest could approach the presence of God in the Temple once each year after a ritual cleansing. Now Jesus is our High Priest,

who declares us to be righteous by faith so that we can now boldly enter into the presence of God at any time and obtain His mercy and His grace!

"For we have not an high priest which cannot be touched with the feeling of our infirmities; but was in all points tempted like as we are, yet without sin. Let us therefore come boldly unto the throne of grace that we may obtain mercy, and find grace to help in time of need." (Hebrews 4:15-16)

## The Different Kinds of Love

The apostle John was known for his abundant love for Jesus and for the brethren. According to the writings of Jerome (CA 347 AD to 430 AD) when John was old he would always greet the brethren by first saying, "Little children, love one another." And in the Scriptures he also identified himself as being the disciple "whom Jesus loved." (John 13:23, 19:26, 20:2, 21:7, 21:20)

He was the only disciple who was not martyred, and he died of natural causes when about ninety-five years old. He was also the only disciple who was given the privilege and the responsibility of taking care of Mary, the natural mother of Jesus.

"When Jesus therefore saw His mother, and the disciple standing by, whom He loved, He saith unto His mother, Woman, behold thy son! Then saith He to the disciple, Behold thy mother! And from that hour that disciple took her unto his own home." (John 19: 26-27)

The New Testament only uses three different Greek words to describe the different kinds of love. The two words most used in the Bible are "agape" and "phileo." The third word "storgay" is only used twice to describe the love for a person's relatives. The "phileo" or friendship kind of love is a good kind of love, but it could change with the circumstances.

The apostle Paul under the inspiration of the Holy Spirit defined the unique "agape" or godly kind of love as follows:

"Love [agape] is patient, love is kind. It does not envy, it does not boast, it is not proud. It is not rude, it is not self-seeking, it is not easily angered, it keeps no records of wrong. Love does not delight in evil but rejoices with the truth. It always protects, always trusts, always hopes, always perseveres." (1 Corinthians 13: 4-7 NIV)

The pure and holy unselfish "agape" and godly kind of love is the best kind of love for it is steadfast and "always protects, always trusts, always hopes, always perseveres."

"And now these three remain: faith, hope and love. But the greatest of these is [agape] love." (1 Corinthians 13:13 NIV)

The best Biblical example to show the difference between the "agape" or unconditional, godly kind of love and the "phileo" or friendship kind of love was when the resurrected Jesus asked His disciple Peter two times if he loved Him while using the "agape" love. And both times Peter responded with the "phileo" love.

Then, on the third time Jesus very kindly switched from His previous request for "agape" love and used the "phileo" love in order to accommodate Peter, who continued to respond with his usual "phileo" love. This revealed the kindness and the compassionate love of Jesus as well as the insecurity of Peter who had previously denied Jesus three times. (Matthew 26:75)

"This is now the third time that Jesus shewed himself to His disciples, after that He was risen from the dead. So when they had dined, Jesus saith to Simon Peter, Simon, son of Jonas, lovest (agape) thou me more than these? He saith unto Him, Yea, Lord; thou knowest that I love (phileo) thee. He saith unto him, Feed my lambs. He saith to him again the second time, Simon, son of Jonas, lovest (agape) thou me? He saith unto Him, Yea, Lord; thou knowest that I love (phileo) thee. He saith unto him, Feed my sheep. He saith unto him the third time, Simon, son of Jonas, lovest (phileo) thou me? Peter was grieved because he said unto Him the third time, Lovest (phileo) thou me? And he said unto Him, Lord, thou knowest all things; thou knowest that I love (phileo) thee. Jesus saith unto him, Feed my sheep." (John 21:14-17)

Before Peter was filled with the "agape" kind of love, he was fearful of what people would think and he even denied knowing Jesus three times. But after he was "filled with the Holy Spirit" he became a leader of the disciples of Jesus and "spoke the word of God boldly" even when he was threatened with prison or physical harm.

"Now, Lord, consider their threats and enable your servants to speak your word with great boldness. Stretch out your hand to heal and perform signs and wonders through the name of your holy servant Jesus." After they prayed, the place where they were meeting was shaken. And they were all filled with the Holy Spirit and spoke the word of God boldly." (Acts 4: 29-31 NIV)

So if you are fearful or overly worried about what people might think more than you are concerned what God might think, then this is a sure sign that you are not fully abiding in the godly kind of love

"There is no fear in love; but perfect love casteth out fear: because fear hath torment. He that feareth is not made perfect in love." (1 John 4:18)

## Sexual Love is to Bear Children

There is actually no word in the Bible to describe sexual love because it only has different words for the kinds of love that are spiritual. Although it can be combined with spiritual love, sexual love is physical and was primarily created by God to bear fruit by the conceiving, bearing, and raising of godly children.

"So God created man in his own image, in the image of God created he him; male and female created he them. And God blessed them, and God said unto them, Be fruitful, and multiply, and replenish the earth, and subdue it: and have dominion over the fish of the sea, and over the fowl of the air, and over every living thing that moveth upon the earth." (Genesis 1: 28-27)

Similar commandments to "be fruitful and multiply and replenish the earth" were also given to both Noah and to Jacob (who was later renamed Israel). All three commandments were given primarily to "replenish the earth" with many godly children.

"And God blessed Noah and his sons, and said unto them, Be fruitful, and multiply, and replenish the earth." (Genesis 9: 1)

"And God said unto him [Israel], I am God Almighty: be fruitful and multiply; a nation and a company of nations shall be of thee, and kings shall come out of thy loins." (Genesis 35: 11)

Sexual love was designed and deliberately made pleasurable by God so that we would multiply and fill the earth. Sexual relations are therefore honorable within a marriage and "the bed undefiled", so there is nothing immoral with enjoying sexual relations even if no children can be conceived. But we are warned that "God will judge" all unmarried fornicators and adulterers who have sexual relations without making the commitment of a marriage.

"Marriage is honorable in all, and the bed undefiled: but whoremongers ['pornos'] and adulterers God will judge." (Hebrews 13:4)

A marriage actually begins when a man and a woman voluntarily make a covenant to leave their parents and to "cleave" together as husband and wife for the rest of their earthly lives. (The Hebrew word for cleave is "dabaq" and it can also mean to cling, stay close, keep close, stick with, or follow closely, etc.)

"And Adam said this is now bone of my bones, flesh of my flesh; she shall be called woman, because she was taken out of man. Therefore shall a man leave his father and mother, and shall cleave to his wife; and they shall be one flesh." (Genesis 2: 23-24)

In Malachi 2:14, God referred to a married woman as "the wife of thy covenant." And in Ezekiel 16:8, God referred to His own marriage covenant with Israel when He said, "Yea, I swore unto thee, and entered into a covenant with thee, and thou becamest mine."

Once a marriage covenant has been made, the man and the woman become "one" in the sight of both God and man. It is the couple's own vows that confirm their lifetime commitment and a priest, minister, or rabbi only witness and legally record it. Therefore marriage vows made before a Justice of the Peace are just as binding in the sight of God.

All children are created as eternal beings, so it is important to have the lifetime marriage commitment made by both their fathers and their mothers in order to assure they will be properly nurtured with love and taught the importance of loving God and others.

"Children, obey your parents in the Lord: for this is right. Honor thy father and mother; which is the first commandment with promise; That it may be well with thee, and thou mayest live long on the earth." (Ephesians 6:1-3, Deuteronomy 5:16)

The importance of raising godly children and of teaching them to "keep the way of the Lord" was also emphasized when the Lord told Abraham why he was going to have a son in his old age.

"For I know him, that he will command his children and his household after him, and they shall keep the way of the Lord, to do justice and judgment; that the Lord may bring upon Abraham that which he hath spoken of him." (Genesis 18:19)

Lust is not love.

"Now to the unmarried [or widowers] and the widows I say: It is good for them to stay unmarried, as I do. But if they cannot control themselves, they should marry, for it is better to marry than to burn with passion." (1 Corinthians 7: 8-9 NIV)

When no marriage commitment has been made between the man and the woman, then any sexual relationship outside of a marriage is considered to be either "fornication" or "adultery." And both of these are strongly condemned by the One who created sex.

- Fornication is defined as any immoral sexual act, and this includes adultery and sexual relations with unmarried persons as well.

- Adultery is defined as sexual intercourse by a married person with someone other than the person's own husband or wife.

Most of what the secular world calls "love" is really "lust". Their hedonistic kind of "love" is often portrayed in the secular media as being a brief sexual encounter without any obligations at all, much less that of a morally binding marriage covenant.

Lust cannot possibly be the same as love, for lust is defined as having excessive or inappropriate desires. And these desires can be for anything, but are usually for money, power, or sex. That is why pastors and church leaders are often warned to avoid the danger of taking "the Gold, the Glory, or the Girls."

Lust has three stages and it begins when a person allows tempting thoughts to enter into his or her mind. Then if these thoughts are allowed to continue, they will become extreme or perverted and sinful desires. And then when these desires are openly expressed in the person's thoughts or actions, they will bring forth spiritual death to the person's soul.

"Let no man say when he is tempted, I am tempted of God; for God cannot be tempted by evil, neither tempteth he any man; but every man is tempted [1] when he is drawn away of his own lust and enticed.

Then [2] when lust has conceived, it bringeth forth sin; and [3] sin, when it is finished, Bridgeforth death!" (James 1: 14-15)

And there is a big difference between the unselfish "agape" kind of love and worldly lust:

- Love seeks the welfare of the other person. Lust seeks only its own self-gratification.
- Love gives without demanding anything in return. Lust demands without giving anything in return.
- Love that is unfulfilled will bring great sorrow. Lust that is unfulfilled will turn into great hate.
- Love will always want to forgive weaknesses. Lust will want to take advantage of weaknesses.

## God's Love Makes Forgiveness Easy

God's love makes it very easy for us to forgive, so the more difficult it is for you to forgive someone, the further you are from the pure love of God. Of course, you can still forgive a person without having any love at all for either God or the person, but this kind of forgiveness is shallow and at best only temporary.

And since unforgiveness is really an example of extreme selfishness and a lack of love for others, then the only permanent cure for unforgiveness must be the unselfish and the pure "agape" kind of love that only comes from God.

"Love [agape] is patient, love is kind. It does not envy, it does not boast, it is not proud. It is not rude, it is not self-seeking, it is not easily angered, it keeps no records of wrong. Love does not delight in evil but rejoices with the truth. It always protects, always trusts, always hopes, always perseveres." (1 Corinthians 13: 4-7 NIV)

If you are still having difficulty in forgiving someone, ask yourself if you really do have this kind of love. Now, have you been patient and kind to the offender, and not rude, proud, self-seeking, or angry? Or are you abiding in God's pure and holy kind of love, for then you will "keep no records of the wrongs" that have been done to you.

When you really love a person, you should find it very easy to forgive and "let it go" and not even bring up the subject again unless there is some unusual reason to do so. And even if the person has not yet repented, you should still love and pray for the person to repent and be forgiven just as the Lord has already forgiven you for your own offenses.

"For if ye forgive men their trespasses, your heavenly Father will also forgive you: But if ye forgive not men their trespasses, neither will your Father forgive your trespasses." (Matthew 6: 14-15)

Again I want to emphasize that when you forgive a person, this does *not* mean that you are justifying the evil that the person has done. It only means that you do not want to hold on to any anger, resentment, or bitterness that will only rob you of your own joy, peace, and prosperity in the Lord.

And once you have the agape love of God in your heart, you will then be able to see the offender as a needy person like you and one who is also imperfect. Then you will be more willing to help the person so that he or she can also receive forgiveness and a spiritual cleansing from all unrighteousness.

"If we confess our sins, He is faithful and just and will forgive us our sins and purify us from all unrighteousness." (1 John 1:9 NIV)

Just saying that you forgive someone without really loving them is most likely not even true. And even if it were true, just "saying" it cannot by itself heal any unforgiveness. In order to be healed of unforgiveness, you should also have genuine love in your heart for the person whom you "say" that you have forgiven.

"Whoever claims to love God yet hates a brother or sister is a liar. For whoever does not love their brother and sister, whom they have seen, cannot love God, whom they have not seen." (1 John 4:20 NIV)

It may take some self-discipline to do this in the beginning, but we all have been given the free will to choose. We can choose life or death, blessings or cursing, goodness or evil, light or darkness, flesh or Spirit, and even forgiveness or unforgiveness.

And God has already loved and forgiven us of our own sins, so it should be a very easy decision to choose to love and forgive others so that we can all "live in peace" with one another.

"Make every effort to live in peace with everyone and to be holy; without holiness no one will see the Lord. See to it that no one falls short of the grace of God and that no bitter root grows up to cause trouble and defile many." (Hebrews 12: 14-15 NIV)


### The Nine Proofs of God's Love


1.  He Gave us Jesus to Redeem us from our Sins

The first and the most obvious proof of God's love is that He loved us so much that even while we were still sinners, He was willing to give us His only beloved Son to take upon Himself the punishment for our sins by suffering and dying upon the cross. This was the only way that God's perfect justice could be satisfied and still justify his forgiveness of our sins.

"For scarcely for a righteous man will one die: yet peradventure for a good man some would even dare to die. But God commendeth his love toward us, in that, while we were yet sinners, Christ died for us. Much more then, being now justified by His blood, we shall be saved from wrath through Him." (Romans 5: 7-9)

And God did not just "loan" us His Son for thirty-three years in order to redeem us and then take Him back to Heaven. When we repented of our sins and believed in the atoning sacrifice of His only begotten Son, He not only forgave us all our sins, but He gave those who received Him the overcoming Spirit of His Son to guide and dwell within us forever.

"For God so loved the world, that he gave his only begotten Son, that whosoever believeth in him should not perish, but have everlasting life." (John 3:16)

## 1. He Blessed Us With Every Blessing in Christ

But then He went even further and the second proof of His love is that even before He laid the foundations of the earth, He foresaw and loved us and "blessed us in the heavenly realms with every spiritual blessing in Christ."

"Praise be to the God and Father of our Lord Jesus Christ, who has blessed us in the heavenly realms with every spiritual blessing in Christ. For he chose us in him before the creation of the world to be holy and blameless in his sight." (Ephesians 1: 3-4 NIV)

As explained earlier, the word "Christ" actually means "the anointing" or "the anointed one" in both the Hebrew and the Greek. Only in eternity will we be able to fully realize just how great all these blessings are, for not only are we forgiven our sins, but Jesus has also paid the price for the healing of our physical bodies and of the mind, will, and emotions of our eternal souls.

"Surely he hath borne our griefs, and carried our sorrows: yet we did esteem him stricken, smitten of God, and afflicted. But he was wounded for our transgressions, he was bruised for our iniquities: the chastisement of our peace was upon him; and with his stripes we are healed." (Isaiah 53: 4-5)

## 2. He Gave the Holy Spirit as a Security Deposit

As a third proof of God's love for us, He has given us the Holy Spirit of Truth as a "deposit" or down payment to guarantee our eternal inheritance with Him. (The word was translated as "earnest" in the King James Version but meant the same thing.)

"When you believed, you were marked in him with a seal, the promised Holy Spirit, who is a deposit guaranteeing our inheritance until the redemption of those who are God's possession—to the praise of his glory." (Ephesians 1: 14-15 NIV)

The benefits of this "deposit" are enormous for they not only include the guarantee of our future inheritance and our eternal life with Him; but also the guarantee that we will receive a new resurrected body; continued forgiveness of any future sins; and restored fellowship with our holy and righteous God.

### 3. He Has Set Us Free from a Guilty Conscience

A fourth proof of God's love is that you no longer have to suffer from a guilty conscience because of your past sins. It almost sounds too good to be true, but when we are in Christ, we are completely free from all guilt and shame because our once defiled human spirit has now been "made alive" by the riches of God's grace, who has "quickened us together with Christ" when He was resurrected from the dead.

"But God, who is rich in mercy, for his great love wherewith he loved us, Even when we were dead in sins, hath quickened us together with Christ, (by grace ye are saved) And hath raised us up together, and made us sit together in heavenly places in Christ Jesus: That in the ages to come he might show the exceeding riches of his grace in his kindness toward us through Christ Jesus." (Ephesians 2: 4-7)

The apostle Paul is a good example of the riches of God's grace. Paul had once caused Christians to be tortured and killed, but after his conversion, he was still able to say to his accusers, "In this do I exercise myself, to have always a conscience void of offense toward God, and toward men." (Acts 24: 16)

"I care very little if I am judged by you or by any human court; indeed, I do not even judge myself. My conscience is clear, but that does not make me innocent. It is the Lord who judges me. Therefore judge nothing before the appointed time; wait till the Lord comes. He will bring to light what is hidden in darkness and will expose the motives of men 's hearts. At that time each will receive his praise from God." (1 Corinthians 4: 3-5 NIV)

## 4.  He Has Made Us New Creations in Christ

A fifth proof of God's love is that He has literally made us completely new creations. We are the first human beings to receive the overcoming Spirit of Christ "within" us and thus be set free from all our sins both now and forever throughout all eternity.

Even though Adam was once made sinless in God's image, he did not have the overcoming spirit of Christ within him for his protection and guidance. However, he probably does now as he most likely received that Spirit of Christ when Jesus preached to the souls in "Abraham's bosom." (I Peter 3:19)

"Therefore if any man be in Christ, he is a new creature: old things are passed away; Behold, all things are become new. And all things are of God, who hath reconciled us to himself by Jesus Christ, and hath given to us the ministry of reconciliation; To wit, that God was in Christ, reconciling the world unto himself not imputing their trespasses unto them; and hath committed unto us the word of reconciliation." (2 Corinthians 5: 17-19)

## 5.  He Made us Holy and Unblameable in His Sight

A sixth proof of God's love for us is that our repentance and confession will always be able to set us free from the righteous judgment of God both now and in the future, even if we should later willfully or intentionally sin.

"Christ hath redeemed us from the curse of the law, being made a curse for us: for it is written, Cursed is every one that hangeth on a tree: That the blessing of Abraham might come on the Gentiles through Jesus Christ; that we might receive the promise of the Spirit through faith." Galatians 3: 13-14)

God loves us so much that even then He is always ready to forgive us. So as long as we rely upon the righteousness of God in Christ and "continue in the faith" then God will continue to see us as being "holy, unblamable, and unreprovable in his sight" and forever free from guilt and condemnation.

"And you that were sometime alienated and enemies in your mind by wicked works, yet now he hath reconciled in the body of his flesh through death, to present you holy, unblameable, and unreprovable in his sight, if you continue in the faith, grounded and settled, and be not moved away from the hope of the gospel." (Colossians 1: 21-23)

6.  He Has Adopted Us As His own Children.

The seventh proof of God's love is that He has agreed to permanently adopt all of us believers who love Jesus into His family as His very own children. This could be the greatest miracle of all.

"But when the set time had fully come, God sent his Son, born of a woman, born under the law, to redeem those under the law, that we might receive adoption to sonship. Because you are his sons, God sent the Spirit of his Son into our hearts, the Spirit who calls out, "Abba, Father. " So you are no longer a slave, but God's child; and since you are his child, God has made you also an heir." (Galatians 4: 4-7 NIV)

The Greek word for "adoption to sonship" was also a legal term for "the full legal standing of an adopted male heir in Roman culture" so this word gives even greater emphasis to the awesome rights and the privileges that we have as sons and daughters of God.

If you have been spiritually reborn by believing in what Jesus Christ has accomplished, then you have been adopted as a "child of God", so the Son of God is not ashamed to call you His own brother or sister!

"Both the one who makes people holy and those who are made holy are of the same family. So Jesus is not ashamed to call them brothers and sisters." (Hebrews 2:11 NIV)

## 7.  He Is Changing Us From Glory To Glory

We are predestined "to be conformed to the image of His Son," and what can be greater proof of God's love for us than having Him continue to change us to be like His Son both now and throughout all eternity?

"And we know that all things work together for good to them that love God, to them who are the called according to his purpose. For whom he did foreknow, he also did predestinate to be conformed to the image of his Son, that he might be the firstborn among many brethren." (Romans 8: 28-29)

When our soul leaves our body, only what He has already changed to be more like Jesus will be resurrected, so we will no longer be sin-conscious. But we will still be growing in the knowledge of God and will continue to be changed "from Glory to Glory" by the Spirit of the Lord.

"Now the Lord is that Spirit: and where the Spirit of the Lord is, there is liberty. But we all, with open face beholding as in a glass the glory of the Lord, are changed into the same image from glory to glory, even as by the Spirit of the Lord." (2 Corinthians 3: 17-18)

### 8. Death Will Soon Be Swallowed Up in Victory

When our physical body dies, our corruptible human body will be left behind and our human spirit will be brought up to Heaven. Our spirit body will at first be like our physical body for "there is a natural body, and there is a spiritual body." (1 Corinthians 15:44)

But during the "catching away" of the church before the time of Jacob's Trouble "when we meet Jesus in the air" (1 Thessalonians 14:15-18) or at another appointed time, we will also have an incorruptible resurrected body. And this body will be like the resurrected body of Jesus that cannot die and that will be when "Death will be swallowed up in Victory!"

"For this corruptible must put on incorruption, and this mortal must put on immortality. So when this corruptible shall have put on incorruption, and this mortal shall have put on immortality, then shall be brought to pass the saying that is written, Death is swallowed up in Victory." (1 Corinthians 15: 53-54)

## Love God with All of your Heart

"In this was manifested the love of God toward us, because that God sent his only begotten Son into the world, that we might live through him. Herein is love, not that we loved God, but that he loved us, and sent his Son to be the propitiation for our sins." (I John 4: 9-10)

The first commandment and what our God wants the most is our worship, which is an intense form of "agape" love. The main reason why God created you and me in His image with free will was so that we could freely love Him back with all of our hearts.

"Yet a time is coming and has now come when the true worshipers will worship the Father in the Spirit and in truth, for they are the kind of worshipers the Father seeks. God is spirit, and his worshipers must worship in the Spirit and in truth." (John 4: 23-24 NIV)

If you do not understand this very basic principle, then you will miss the whole point of why you were created, and you may even end up legalistically trying to please Him with your own works when all that He really wants is your *love*.

"If I speak in the tongues of men or of angels, but do not have [agape] love, I am only a resounding gong or a clanging cymbal. If I have the gift of prophecy and can fathom all mysteries and all knowledge, and if I have a faith that can move mountains, but do not have love, I am nothing. If I give all I possess to the poor and give over my body to hardship that I may boast, but do not have love, I gain nothing." (1 Corinthians 13: 1-3 NIV)

This is why there are so many legalistic preachers who are trying to get their congregations to please God by their own works, when God has already been com-pletely satisfied by the love and the sacrifice of His only begotten Son, Jesus Christ.

In short, there is nothing more that we can do on our own that exceeds the love and the sacrifice of Jesus. So the only works we can do now that please Him are to obey him and "worship Him in spirit and truth" and then only do the works that He has inspired.

When Jesus was asked what the greatest commandment in the Law of Moses was, He replied that it was to love God with all of your heart, soul, and mind. (Deuteronomy 6:5) But then He went beyond the original question and added another love commandment to "love your neighbor as yourself."

"Jesus said unto him, Thou shalt love the Lord thy God with all thy heart, and with all thy soul, and with all thy mind. This is the first and great commandment. And the second is like unto it, Thou shalt love thy neighbor as thyself On these two commandments hang all the law and the prophets." (Matthew 22: 37-40)

Perhaps the most important words in this passage are when Jesus said, "On these two commandments [i.e. loving God and loving our neighbor] hang all the law and the prophets." This means that loving God and our fellow man is our main purpose while we are still here on this earth and later for all eternity.

And once we have Christ in us, the hope of glory, it is definitely not the legalistic observation of a system of laws, rules, and regulations which were given under the Law of Moses.

"Therefore do not let anyone judge you by what you eat or drink, or with regard to a religious festival, a New Moon celebration or a Sabbath day. These are a shadow of the things that were to come; the reality, however, is found in Christ." (Colossians 2: 16-17 NIV)

When Jesus spoke about loving God as being the greatest of all the commandments, He first mentioned loving God with all of your heart which is your innermost being that includes both your eternal soul and your mind.

Then He spoke about loving God more specifically with the mind, will, and emotions of your eternal soul, which is the "real you" and this includes your unique personality and your own personal desires.

Then He spoke about loving God specifically with the intimate thoughts and the intents of your mind. This seems to imply that the most effective expression of our love for our Creator is with the thoughts and the intents in each of our own minds, for this is where we express our most intimate feelings and desires.

And Jesus most likely put loving God and loving your neighbor together because you cannot fully love God if you do not fully love your neighbor. This is because God also loves that person too, no matter what he or she might have done in the past, for all sins can be covered by His love, mercy, and grace.

"We love because he first loved us. Whoever claims to love God yet hates a brother or sister is a liar. For whoever does not love their brother and sister, whom they have seen, cannot love God, whom they have not seen. And he has given us this command: Anyone who loves God must also love their brother and sister." (1 John 4: 19-21 NIV)

Apparently the first century church at Ephesus was doing just about everything else right, but in the midst of their trials they had "forsaken their first love." Jesus said that if they did not repent and return to their first love, He would have to remove His presence from their assemblies.

This scripture may also explain why His presence is no longer known, even in many churches today.

"You have persevered and have endured hardships for my name and have not grown weary. Yet I hold this against you: You have forsaken the love you had at first. Consider how far you have fallen! Repent and do the things you did at first. If you do not repent, I will come to you and remove your lampstand from its place." (Revelation 2: 3-5 NIV)

## Love and Forgive your Neighbor

The second most important love commandment is to "love your neighbor as yourself." When you really do love your neighbor with the love of God, then you should not have any problem at all with also forgiving your neighbor.

"Dear friends, let us love one another, for love comes from God. Everyone who loves has been born of God and knows God. Whoever does not love does not know God, because God is love. This is how God showed his love among us: He sent his one and only Son into the world that we might live through him. This is love: not that we loved God, but that he loved us and sent his Son as an atoning sacrifice for our sins." (1 John 4: 7-10 NIV)

And since God has forgiven all who love Him and does not bring up our own past sins, we should do the same with each other. For when we forgive others as we would also like to be forgiven, then it is just as if the offenses had never even happened. And then true love for one another can flourish once more.

The best example of unselfish love and forgiveness is, of course, our own Lord and Savior, Jesus Christ, who loves us all, both the good and bad, and He is always willing to forgive anyone who repents and comes to Him. And the more we become like Him, the greater will be our love.

"All that the Father giveth me shall come to me; and him that cometh to me I will in no wise cast out. For I came down from heaven, not to do mine own will, but the will of him that sent me." (John 6: 37-38)

We are all imperfect human beings, so the key to happiness is really not how much you know, but rather how much you love and are able to forgive. All you have to do is forgive and hopefully release the person from the consequences that would otherwise result from the bad behavior.

When we live for God and forgive and help others, we demonstrate our love for God, while at the same time we reveal the love of God to those whom we help. Most of us do not have high profile ministries, but we all have someone whom we can help.

"This is how we know what love is: Jesus Christ laid down his life for us. And we ought to lay down our lives for our brothers and sisters. If anyone has material possessions and sees a brother or sister in need but has no pity on them, how can the love of God be in that person? Dear children, let us not love with words or speech but with actions and in truth." (1 John 3: 16-18 NIV)

When you really love God and your fellow man with "actions and in truth," there are many things that God might inspire you to do to help others.

You could visit a neighbor, make new friends, pray for the sick, comfort those in nursing homes, provide meals for shut-ins, help the unemployed become self-supporting, visit or write to prisoners, do or support missionary work, help out at a soup kitchen, help support those that feed and clothe the poor, sing in the choir, teach in Sunday School, or maybe even move to a better location and join a new church.

"Then Jesus said to his host, "When you give a luncheon or dinner, do not invite your friends, your brothers or sisters, your relatives, or your rich neighbors; if you do, they may invite you back and so you will be repaid. But when you give a banquet, invite the poor, the crippled, the lame, the blind, and you will be blessed. Although they cannot repay you, you will be repaid at the resurrection of the righteous." (Luke 14: 12-14 NIV)

And don't think that God has forgotten about your own desires. He takes great pleasure in the prosperity of His servants so you can expect Him to also inspire you to do new things that will benefit your own life as well that "your joy will be complete."

"In that day you will no longer ask me anything. Very truly I tell you, my Father will give you whatever you ask in my name. Until now you have not asked for anything in my name. Ask and you will receive, and your joy will be complete." (John 16: 23-24 NIV)

Who is my Neighbor?

When Jesus was asked, "What must I do to inherit eternal life?" Jesus answered, "What is written in the Law?" The man replied, "Love the Lord your God with all your heart and with all your soul and with all your strength and with all your mind; and to love your neighbor as yourself."

Jesus said he had answered correctly. But in order to justify himself, the man asked, "Who is my neighbor?"

In reply Jesus said: "A man was going down from Jerusalem to Jericho, when he was attacked by robbers. They stripped him of his clothes, beat him and went away, leaving him halfdead. A priest happened to be going down the same road, and when he saw the man, he passed by on the other side.

So too, a Levite, when he came to the place and saw him, passed by on the other side. But a Samaritan, as he traveled, came where the man was; and when he saw him, he took pity on him.

He went to him and bandaged his wounds, pouring on oil and wine. Then he put the man on his own donkey, brought him to an inn and took care of him. The next day he took out two denarii and gave them to the innkeeper. 'Look after him', he said, 'and when I return, I will reimburse you for any extra expense you may have.'

Which of these three do you think was a neighbor to the man who fell into the hands of robbers?"

The expert in the law replied, "The one who had mercy on him. " Jesus told him, "Go and do likewise." (Luke 10: 30-37 NIV)

## Love and Forgive Yourself

Perhaps there should have been a third love commandment, for it is virtually im-possible to love God and others completely if we do not even love ourselves. If you feel that way, then I want to remind you that Jesus said we were to love others as we love ourselves, so it must be God's will to love ourselves.

"Jesus replied, 'You shall not murder, you shall not commit adultery, you shall not steal, you shall not give false testimony, honor your father and mother and love your neighbor as yourself." (Matthew 19: 18-19 NIV)

Loving and feeling good about yourself is not necessarily vain or prideful as long as it is linked together with humility, gratitude, and a sincere love for God and others. In other words, your love has to be the unselfish "agape" kind of love, for this is the only kind of love that will produce a healthy self-esteem without turning into vanity or pride.

When you abide in the godly "agape" kind of love and focus your thoughts on loving and serving God, as well as loving and helping one another unselfishly with His perfect love, then your self-esteem can be at brought up to its highest level. And you would also be bearing good fruit and giving God all the glory for how He has changed your life.

On this subject I'll address a few points.

1.  Don't Be Intimidated.

Sometimes people are not able to forgive themselves because they have been intimidated, brainwashed, bullied, abused, and lied to until they think that they are to blame for everything bad that has befallen them. And even if this were true, it really would not matter if they have repented and been forgiven of their sins. (1 John 1:9)

If you once had an abortion and killed an innocent baby in the womb, then this act can cause feelings of shame to linger for a lifetime. But even this can turn into joy when you realize that your child has since been growing up in Heaven and that he or she is now looking forward to meeting you for the first time.

And others may still feel ashamed because of what they have done in the past and blame themselves until they feel worthless. The greatest feelings of shame usually come from a variety of sexual or drug addictions. The solution is to "despise the shame" for we are all sinners saved by grace and look unto Jesus who, "for the joy set before him endured the cross, despising the shame."

"Looking unto Jesus the author and finisher of our faith; who for the joy that was set before him endured the cross, despising the shame, and is set down at the right hand of the throne of God." (Hebrews 12: 2)

Continuing to blame yourself for past mistakes after converting to Christ is really a subtle form of self-righteous pride and deception, because we all have made mis-takes. And worse yet, it denies the fact that God remembers our sins no more, for Jesus has "washed us from our sins in his own blood" and has made us "kings and priests unto God and his Father."

"And from Jesus Christ, who is the faithful witness, and the first begotten of the dead, and the prince of the kings of the earth. Unto him that loved us, and washed us from our sins in his own blood, And hath made us kings and priests unto God and his Father; to him be glory and dominion for ever and ever. Amen." (Revelation 1: 5-6)

## 2.  The so-called "Unforgivable Sin"

There may be a few who cannot forgive themselves because they "think" that they might have committed the so-called "un-forgivable sin." The short answer is that if you are worried about it, then you have *not* committed it. For if you had done it, you would not know it, as you would then be in unbelief like the Pharisees in Matthew 12, Mark 3, and Luke 12.

In addition, the Pharisees who blas-phemed the Holy Spirit were still under the Old Covenant and had even accused Jesus of being "the prince of devils." They did not believe the good news of the Gospel and had even said that the gifts of the Holy Spirit were really the works of evil demons.

And now we are under a new and a much better Covenant of Grace, where all sins     are forgivable, including even blasphemy or speaking against the Holy Spirit, for "the blood of Jesus Christ his Son cleanseth us from *all* sin."

"If we say that we have fellowship with him, and walk in darkness, we lie, and do not the truth: But if we walk in the light, as he is in the light, we have fellowship one with another, and the blood of Jesus Christ his Son cleanseth us from all sin." (1 John 1: 6-7)

### 3.  God is Always Good and Fair

We all have done things we are not proud of, so the reason why some Christians find it difficult to forgive themselves may be because they cannot fully comprehend the depth of just how good our God really is. He is so com-pletely "all good" that there is not even a trace of sinful thoughts in Him for, "God is light" and "in him there is no darkness at all."

"This is the message we have heard from him and declare to you: God is light; in him there is no darkness at all. If we claim to have fellowship with him and yet walk in the darkness, we lie and do not live out the truth. But if we walk in the light, as he is in the light, we have fellowship with one another, and the blood of Jesus, his Son, purifies us from all sin." (1 John: 5-7NIV)

Our God loves us all very intensely and already has a wonderful plan for each of our lives. He is really a lot like the father of        the prodigal son who loved his son un-conditionally. He holds no grudges, and He rejoices greatly whenever a wayward son or daughter repents.

So no matter what things you may have done in your past, you never have to be ashamed, for Jesus has already born your shame and put it to death upon the cross. And as long as you have true repentance, your heavenly Father still love you and will always forgive you and welcome you back into His holy presence.

"But we do see Jesus, who was made lower than the angels for a little while, now crowned with glory and honor because he suffered death, so that by the grace of God he might taste death for everyone. In bringing many sons and daughters to glory, it was fitting that God, for whom and through whom everything exists, should make the pioneer of their salvation perfect through what he suffered. Both the one who makes people holy and those who are made holy are of the same family. So Jesus is not ashamed to call them brothers and sisters." (Hebrews 2: 9-11)

### 4. How to Overcome Rejection

Rejection is the act of discarding someone as being completely worthless or incompetent, and it can be done with a look of disdain or a gesture, but it is usually expressed by the speaking or the writing of words that are filled with condemnation.

Maybe you have a low self-esteem and do not love yourself because you do not know how to cope with the personal rejection that comes from insensitive and spiritually ignorant people.

While rejection for the sake of the Gospel will yield an eternal reward, personal rejection can shatter your self-esteem and keep you from receiving the fullness of our Lord's blessings. But you can overcome the negative words with the Truth, for the words of God are the antidote for all the negative words or actions, including personal rejection.

And the Bible says that your God loves you so much that He was willing to sacrifice His only begotten Son, whom He loved very deeply, just so that you and I could be re-deemed from our sins and have intimate fellowship with Him throughout all eternity.

And the Bible also says that Jesus Christ loves you so much that He was willing to leave His heavenly father and become a mortal human being just so He could pay the price for our redemption by suffering and ultimately dying on a cross.

Now that is certainly a lot of unconditional love that our God and His Son have for you and I, and it is all without even the slightest hint of any condemnation. For if you are a true believer in Jesus Christ, then God has already forgiven your past, present, and future sins because of what Jesus has accomplished.

"There is therefore now no condemnation to them which are in Christ Jesus, who walk not after the flesh, but after the Spirit. For the law of the Spirit of life in Christ Jesus hath made me free from the law of sin and death. For what the law could not do, in that it was weak through the flesh, God sending his own Son in the likeness of sinful flesh, and for sin, condemned sin in the flesh: That the righteousness of the law might be fulfilled in us, who walk not after the flesh, but after the Spirit." (Romans 8: 1-4)

## To Love and Forgive our Enemies

"You have heard that it was said, 'Love your neighbor and hate your enemy. ' But I tell you, love your enemies and pray for those who persecute you, that you may be children of your Father in heaven. He causes his sun to rise on the evil and the good, and sends rain on the righteous and the unrighteous. If you love those who love you, what reward will you get? Are not even the tax collectors doing that? And if you greet only your own people, what are you doing more than others? Do not even pagans do that? Be perfect, therefore, as your heavenly Father is perfect." (Mathew 5: 43-48 NIV)

Few people realize that under the Law of Moses, the Israelites were permitted to hate their enemies, for they worshipped false gods. But under this same Law, the Israelites still had to forgive their brethren and could not hold any grudges or seek any revenge among their own relatives. And they also had to love their Israeli neighbors as themselves.

"Do not hate a fellow Israelite in your heart. Rebuke your neighbor frankly so you will not share in their guilt. Do not seek revenge or bear a grudge against anyone among your people, but love your neighbor as yourself. I am the LORD." (Leviticus 19: 17-18 NIV)

Why the difference?

We are now under the New Covenant of Grace, and the redemptive sacrifice of Jesus has now been made available to all nations, both Jewish and Gentile. This is why we are to love and forgive even our enemies, for they now have the potential to become our friends by the same saving grace we have received as believers in Jesus Christ.

"If you love those who love you, what credit is that to you? Even sinners love those who love them. And if you do good to those who are good to you, what credit is that to you? Even sinners do that. And if you lend to those from whom you expect repayment, what credit is that to you? Even sinners lend to sinners, expecting to be repaid in full. But love your enemies, do good to them, and lend to them without expecting to get anything back. Then your reward will be great, and you will be children of the Most High, because he is kind to the ungrateful and wicked. Be merciful, just as your Father is merciful." (Luke 6: 32-36 NIV)

At first it may be difficult to even think of loving your enemies or doing good to those who hate you. But if you will continue to spend time abiding in the love of God, you will soon see your enemy from His perspective. You will then be able to share in His compassion for the lost, and it will be much easier to love and forgive even your worst enemies.

If you love and intercede for your enemies, this is what opens the door for God to reveal to you His perspective and His very great love for those who are lost. When you love, bless, and pray for your enemies, you are then "not overcome of evil, but overcome evil with good." (Romans 12:21)

"Bless those who persecute you; bless and do not curse. Rejoice with those who rejoice; mourn with those who mourn. Live in harmony with one another. Do not be proud, but be willing to associate with people ofl ow position. Do not be conceited. Do not repay anyone evil for evil. Be careful to do what is right in the eyes of everyone. If it is possible, as far as it depends on you, live at peace with everyone. Do not take revenge, my dear friends, but leave room for God's wrath, for it is written: "It is mine to avenge; I will repay", says the Lord." (Romans 12: 14-19 NIV)

As indicated at the end of the previous scripture, if your enemies do not repent, it will be impossible for them to escape from the judgment of God. But if they do repent and become believers, they will be forgiven by the grace and the mercy of God, and you will then be very glad that you had loved and prayed for them.

"For if God spared not the natural branches, take heed lest he also spare not thee. Behold therefore the goodness and severity of God: on them which fell, severity; but toward thee, goodness, if thou continue in his goodness: otherwise thou also shalt be cut off. And they also, if they abide not still in unbelief, shall be grafted in: for God is able to graft them in again." (Romans 11: 21-23)

Another way to look at your enemies is to realize that God is able to work even bad things together for good by using them to make us more conformed to the image of His Son. But this will only be true for the believers who really do love Him and are "called according to his purpose."

So your enemies will still have to repent and become believers before they will be able to benefit from the goodness of God.

"And we know that all things work together for good to them that love God, to them who are called according to his purpose. For whom he did foreknow, he also did predestinate to be conformed to the image of his Son, that he might be the firstborn among many brethren." (Romans 8: 28-29)

Joseph is an excellent example of this, for he was so hated by his brothers that they even tried to kill him. But he was instead sold into slavery where he was tempted and tested. After he was proven faithful, he went from prison to the throne of Egypt and forgave his brothers of their evil deeds, for he could then see how God had worked so much good out of their evil.

"And Joseph said unto them, Fear not: for am I in the place of God? But as for you, ye thought evil against me; but God meant it unto good, to bring to pass, as it is this day, to save much people alive." (Genesis 50: 19-20)

You will know that you are also completely free from unforgiveness when you can see how God is working good out of their evil and you now only have love, compassion, and mercy for those who were once your enemies.

And don't be surprised if you should find yourself not only forgiving them, but also praying and earnestly interceding for all who had once been considered your enemies, for that is what you do when you really love someone.

"The end of all things is near. Therefore be alert and of sober mind so that you may pray. Above all, love each other deeply, because love covers over a multitude of sins. Offer hospitality to one another without grumbling. Each of you should use whatever gift you have received to serve others, as faithful stewards of God's grace in its various forms." (1 Peter 4: 7-10 NIV)

## Love Increases with Forgiveness

Whenever people have been forgiven a lot of offenses, they will almost always be extremely grateful and have even greater love for all who had forgiven them. Jesus revealed this in the following true story that whoever has been forgiven much will then love even more.

"A woman in that town who lived a sinful life learned that Jesus was eating at the Pharisee's house, so she came there with an alabaster jar of perfume. As she stood behind him at his feet weeping, she began to wet his feet with her tears. Then she wiped them with her hair, kissed them and poured perfume on them." (Luke 7: 37-38 NIV)

The Pharisee who had invited Jesus to the dinner was embarrassed by the woman's behavior and thought that if Jesus were a true prophet, He would have known this woman was a sinner, so Jesus said to him:

"Do you see this woman? I came into your house. You did not give me any water for my feet, but she wet my feet with her tears and wiped them with her hair. You did not give me a kiss, but this woman, from the time I entered, has not stopped kissing my feet. You did not put oil on my head, but she has poured perfume on my feet. Therefore, I tell you, her many sins have been forgiven — as her great love has shown. But whoever has been forgiven little loves little." Then Jesus said to her, "Your sins are forgiven." (Luke 7: 44-48 NIV)

I remember reading about a former prostitute who was led to the Lord through a Christian evangelistic ministry. Later she met and married a wonderful Christian man. Her husband loved his wife so much and he was so grateful that he would write the ministry every year just to thank them. He just wanted to let them know how much he appreciated what they and the Lord had done for both of them.

That is only one example of the life changing grace and love of almighty God. He is able to transform a life that had once been destroyed by sin and make it into a new and a much more abundant life.

"The thief cometh not, but for to steal, and to kill, and to destroy: I am come that they might have life, and that they might have it more abundantly. I am the good shepherd: the good shepherd giveth his life for the sheep." (John 10: 10-11)

The godly "agape" kind of love as defined by the apostle Paul is always ready to forgive and forget the past for the divine punishment has already been paid by our Lord and Savior, Jesus Christ.

"Love [agape] is patient, love is kind. It does not envy, it does not boast, it is not proud. It is not rude, it is not self-seeking, it is not easily angered, it keeps no records of wrongs. Love does not delight in evil but rejoices with the truth. It always protects, always trusts, always hopes, always perseveres." (1 Corinthians 13: 4-7 NIV)

Within this definition of love, there are many other qualities that should be in all of us when we forgive even our enemies. Two of the most important qualities that relate to forgiveness are that love "is kind" and that it "keeps no records of wrongs."

Some of the other important qualities are that love is "not self-seeking" and only "rejoices with the truth." And it "always perseveres" and, of course, it will not even show a hint of having any "boasting" or "pride."

And one of the most important things to remember forever is located at the end of the so-called "love chapter." It is that even in eternity after this earth is replaced with a new earth, these three-character traits will still remain: They are "faith, hope and love, but the greatest of these is love."

"For now we see only a reflection as in a mirror; then we shall see face to face. Now I know in part; then I shall know fully, even as I am fully known. And now these three remain: faith, hope and love. But the greatest of these is love." (1 Corinthians 13: 12-13)

## The Love of Karla Faye Tucker

Karla Fay Tucker was not always full of the love of God, and she had once actively participated in a botched burglary with two friends which became one of the most violent and evil murders in history. She had been on mind altering drugs at the time, but she was still guilty of an extremely despicable crime.

She was dramatically converted to Christianity while she was still in the prison awaiting her execution.

Her (as I see it) genuine repentance, and her manifest love for Jesus was so complete that she became a model prisoner during the fourteen years that she was still on death row.

She was witnessing the love of Jesus to the other inmates and visitors and her steadfast "agape" love for her Lord and fellow inmates was so complete that her attorneys sought the commutation of her sentence from death to life in prison. And the legality of her case was even reviewed by the U S Supreme Court, although it ruled against her without comment.

Karla Faye was so effective in witnessing the love of Jesus both inside and outside the prison (by way of the secular media) that her supporters included the United Nations Commissioner on "summary and arbitrary executions", Pope John Paul II, the World Council of Churches, evangelist Pat Robertson, Senator Newt Gingrich, and many others, including myself.

There was also an appeal to the then Texas Governor, George W. Bush for the commutation of her death sentence to life imprisonment. This was, of course, before he became President of the United States.

In response to my own appeal for mercy, I received a signed letter from George W. Bush explaining why he believed he should not commute her sentence and why he should allow the legal execution to continue.

I still have that letter and I have included a copy of it in the appendix of this book. While I did not agree with his decision, I did not question his motivation. And God may have wanted Karla Fay to be taken up to Heaven while she was still at the peak of her spiritual growth.

Her execution was done by lethal injection, and it was televised. The people on one side were those who still hated her and could never forgive her for what she had done. They only wanted revenge and were very angry and bitter. Some of them even hurled angry insults at Karla Fay while she was dying.

But those on the other side loved her and had long ago forgiven her, including even the husband and a brother of one of her victims. And just before her soul was brought up to Heaven by the angels, she spoke to those who loved and had forgiven her.

The following were her last words as quoted and recorded in an article about her life:

"Yes sir, I would like to say to all of you the Thornton family and Jerry Dean's family — that I am so sorry. I hope God will give you peace with this. (She looked at her husband) Baby, I love you. (She looked at Ronald Carlson) Ron, give Pego a hug for me. (She looked at all present weeping and smiling) Everybody has been so good to me. I love all of you very much. I am going to be face to face with Jesus now. Warden Baggett, thank all of you so much. You have been so good to me. I love all of you very much. I will see you all when you get there. I will wait for you."

## Be Filled with the Holy Spirit

We can all be filled with the Holy Spirit and there are no limitations on how much we can receive. And this is such an enormous privilege that it is difficult for our finite human minds to comprehend it, for the Holy Spirit is so holy that, without the sacrifice of Jesus, we wouldn't even be able to get near Him, much less have close and intimate fellowship with Him.

"Wherefore be ye not unwise but understanding what the will of the Lord is. And be not drunk with wine, wherein is excess; but be filled with the Spirit." (Ephesians 5: 17-18)

The Holy Spirit will always glorify our Lord Jesus Christ. He "will guide you into all truth" and will even "show you things to come." He is very symbolic and often speaks to us in enigmas, similitude, visions, and dreams, etc., as well as directly through the gifts of the Holy Spirit. (1 Corinthians 12:8-10)

"Howbeit when he, the Spirit of truth, is come, he will guide you into all truth: for he shall not speak of himself; but whatsoever he shall hear, that shall he speak: and he will show you things to come. He shall glorify me: for he shall receive of mine and shall show it unto you." (John 16: 13-14)

The Holy Spirit is a separate person in our Triune God, who proceeds directly from the Father. He is our own personal Comforter and the Spirit of Truth who confirms to us the truth that Jesus Christ is the only begotten Son of God and the only way to the Father.

"But when the Comforter is come, whom I will send unto you from the Father, even the Spirit of truth, which proceedeth from the Father, he shall testify of me" (John 15: 26)

The Holy Spirit is also our teacher who will teach us all things that are important for us to know and will bring the words that Jesus has already spoken to our remembrance whenever they are needed.

"But the Comforter, which is the Holy Ghost, whom the Father will send in my name, he shall teach you all things, and bring all things to your remembrance, whatsoever I have said unto you." (John 14: 26)

The Holy Spirit is our own personal "Comforter" and the "Spirit of Truth" but His main ministry at this present time is to move upon the lost and to "reprove the world of sin, and of righteousness, and of judgment" (John 16: 7-11) for no one can come to Jesus unless the Father "draws him" by His Spirit.

"No man can come to me, [Jesus] except the Father which hath sent me draw him: and I will raise him up at the last day." (John 6: 44)

Jesus told a Samaritan woman that God is a Spirit and that He actively seeks those who will worship Him. So in order to be filled with the Spirit, we must praise and worship God "in spirit and in truth" for He knows the thoughts and the intents of all our hearts.

"But the hour cometh and now is, when the true worshippers shall worship the Father in spirit and in truth: for the Father seeketh such to worship him. God is a Spirit: and they that worship him must   worship him in spirit and in truth." (John 4: 23-24)

When we praise and worship the Father "in spirit and in truth" and do His will, He then sends His Holy Spirit to respond to our love by filling us to overflowing with His awesome presence. Our human spirits and our souls are then flooded with the "righteousness, peace, and joy in the Holy Spirit."

"For the kingdom of God is not a matter of eating and drinking, but of righteousness, peace and joy in the Holy Spirit." (Romans 14: 17 NIV)

All truly "born again" Christians have a portion of the Holy Spirit within them for "the fullness of the Godhead dwells in Christ." And when we are "filled with the Spirit", an abundance of the Holy Spirit's presence can also overflow and bless others as well.

Of course, both the Father and His Son are presently located in a place we call Heaven, but we are still able to have intimate fellowship and communion with them by way of the Holy Spirit, for He also acts as the emissary for both the Father and the Son.

The actual presence of the Holy Spirit will leave if He is grieved by such things as "bitterness, rage and anger, brawling and slander, along with every form of malice " and you may even lose your reward for the good works that you have already done.

"Do not let any unwholesome talk come out of your mouths, but only what is helpful for building others up according to their needs, that it may benefit those who listen. And do not grieve the Holy Spirit of God, with whom you were sealed for the day of redemption. Get rid of all bitterness, rage and anger, brawling and slander, along with every form of malice." (Ephesians 4: 29-31 NIV)

But Jesus and the Holy Sprit within the Spirit of Christ will not leave even if you are sometimes not living righteously. So you don't have to be fearful, for as long as you want and love Jesus, God the Father will always love you.

"Jesus answered and said unto him, If a man love me, he will keep my words: and my Father will love him, and we will come unto him, and make our abode with him." (John 14: 23)

So if you are very wise and want to be blessed with even more of His Glory and His "righteousness, peace, and joy in the Holy Spirit," then you will turn away from anything that might grieve the Holy Spirit and abide in His perfect love.

## His Love is Freedom

"Love worketh no ill to his neighbor: therefore love is the fulfilling of the law." (Romans 13: 10)

When we abide in the Spirit of our Lord, we also abide in His love and in His righteousness. As long as we are abiding in him; we are free from all of our sinful desires including any unforgiveness or bitterness, for "in him there is no sin." This is very important to remember for we are all prone to sin.

"And ye know that he was manifested to take away our sins; and in him is no sin. Whosoever abideth in him sinneth not: whosoever sinneth hath not seen him, neither known him. Little children, let no man deceive you: he that doeth righteousness is righteous, even as he is righteous." (1 John 3: 5-7)

If you have been "born again" by believing in and confessing your faith in Jesus Christ as your own Lord and Savior, then you should also have the Spirit of Christ already abiding within your human spirit (Colossians 1 :27) as well as the perfect mind of Christ. (1 Corinthians 2:16)

Since the Spirit of Christ indwells in all true believers, and Jesus is one with His Father, God has already raised us up and "seated us with him in the heavenly realms in Christ Jesus." Therefore when we abide in the Spirit of Christ, we are also spiritually seated with Jesus next to His Father and are therefore also able to partake of "the incomparable riches of his grace."

"But because of his great love for us, God, who is rich in mercy, made us alive with Christ even when we were dead in transgressions — it is by grace you have been saved. And God raised us up with Christ and seated us with him in the heavenly realms in Christ Jesus, in order that in the coming ages he might show the incomparable riches of his grace, expressed in his kindness to us in Christ Jesus." (Ephesians 2: 4-7 NIV)

In the following Scripture, Jesus compared Himself to being the true vine and His Father like a gardener who prunes the branches so that they can bear more fruit. And we are like the branches which must abide in the vine and be constantly pruned by our heavenly Father so we can bear more fruit.

"I am the true vine, and my Father is the gardener. He cuts off every branch in me that bears no fruit, while every branch that does bear fruit, he prunes so that it will be even more fruitful. You are already clean because of the word I have spoken to you. Remain in me, as I also remain in you. No branch can bear fruit by itself; it must remain in the vine. Neither can you bear fruit unless you remain in me." (John 15: 1-4)

And when we abide in His love and obey His instructions, we will abide in the light of God that gives us understanding of all things. "But anyone who hates a brother or sister is in the darkness" and the hate in them will blind their senses.

"Anyone who claims to be in the light but hates a brother or sister is still in the darkness. Anyone who loves their brother and sister lives in the light, and there is nothing in them to make them stumble. But anyone who hates a brother or sister is in the darkness and walks around in the darkness. They do not know where they are going, because the darkness has blinded them." (1 John 2: 9-11 NIV)

If you want to know if you are abiding in His Spirit, then all you have to do is give yourself a "spiritual fruit test." The word "flesh" is used to describe our carnal nature, and the capitalized word "Spirit" is used to describe the Spirit of Christ which abides in all who have been 'born again."

"For, brethren, ye have been called unto liberty; only use not liberty for an occasion to the flesh, but by love serve one another. For all the law is fulfilled in one word, even in this; Thou shalt love thy neighbor as thyself." (Galatians 5: 13-14)

When you only follow your own fleshly desires you will not be able to abide in His perfect love. But if you yield to the Spirit within you, and do what He inspires you to do, then you will be able to abide in Him and manifest the fruit of the Spirit.

"The acts of the flesh are obvious: sexual immorality, impurity and debauchery; idolatry and witchcraft; hatred, discord, jealousy, fits of rage, selfish ambition, dissensions, factions and envy; drunkenness, orgies, and the like. I warn you, as I did before, that those who live like this will not inherit the kingdom of God.

But the fruit of the Spirit is love, joy, peace, forbearance, kindness, goodness, faithfulness, gentleness and self-control. Against such things there is no law. Those who belong to Christ Jesus have crucified the flesh with its passions and desires. Since we live by the Spirit, let us keep in step with the spirit." (Galatians 5: 16-25 NIV)

Now the question to ask your self is, "Am I just following the selfish desires of my own flesh and bearing the bad fruit that hurts or offends people? Or am I being led by the precious Holy Spirit and bearing the good fruit of righteousness that will always bless people and glorify God?

"By their fruit you will recognize them. Do people pick grapes from thorn bushes, or figs from thistles? Likewise, every good tree bears good fruit, but a bad tree bears bad fruit. A good tree cannot bear bad fruit, and a bad tree cannot bear good fruit. Every tree that does not bear good fruit is cut down and thrown into the fire. Thus, by their fruit you will recognize them." (Mathew 7: 16-25 NIV)

"And this is love: that we walk in obedience to his commands. you have heard from the beginning; his command is that you walk in love." (2 John 1: 6)

Of course, we must continue to walk in His love and be obedient to our Lord's commands if we are to remain free. And it is not always easy to "walk in love" while we are still living in the midst of this corrupt and sinful world. For in it is "the lust of the flesh, the lust of the eyes, and the pride of life."

"Do not love the world or anything in the world. If anyone loves the world, love for the Father is not in them. For everything in the world—the lust of the flesh, the lust of the eyes, and the pride of life—comes not from the Father but from the world. The world and its desires pass away, but whoever does the will of God lives forever." (1 John 2: 15-17 NIV)

And these are "perilous times" because we are now very near the end of the "last days" which precede the "catching away" of the saints before great tribulation and the soon return of our Lord Jesus Christ, who will rule and reign over the entire earth for one thousand years. (Revelation 20:4)

"This know also, that in the last days perilous times shall come. For men shall be lovers of their own selves, covetous, boasters, proud, blasphemers, disobedient to parents, unthankful, unholy, With-out natural affection, trucebreakers, false accusers, incontinent, fierce, despisers of those that are good, Traitors, heady, high-minded, lovers of pleasures more than lovers of God; Having a form of godliness, but denying the power thereof: from such turn away." (2 Timothy 3: 1-5)

One of many reasons why God has given us the overcoming Spirit of His Son while we are still on the earth is so that we can be "partakers of His divine nature" and thus escape from the corruption that is in this world. For when we submit ourselves unto God and resist the devil, he will have to flee. (James 4:7)

"Finally, my brethren, be strong in the Lord, and in the power of his might. Put on the whole armor of God, that ye may be able to stand against the wiles of the devil. For we wrestle not against flesh and blood, but against principalities, against powers, against the rulers of the darkness of this world, against spiritual wickedness in high places." (Ephesians 6: 10-12)

And the Holy Spirit and the fullness of the Godhead that is in the Spirit of Christ will help us "walk in love" so that we can continue to remain free from the obvious "corruption that is in the world through lust."

"Whereby are given unto us exceeding great and precious promises: that by these ye might be partakers of the divine nature, having escaped the corruption that is in the world through lust." (2 Peter 1: 4)

If we "keep his commandments and do the things that are pleasing in his sight" we shall receive whatever we ask. But these are not the commandments in the Law of Moses, for the New Covenant requirements are to love and obey God and to "believe on the name of his Son Jesus Christ, and to love one another."

"And whatsoever we ask, we receive of him, because we keep his commandments, and do those things that are pleasing in his sight. And this is his commandment: That we should believe on the name of his Son Jesus

Christ, and love one another, as he gave us commandment." (1 John 3: 22-23)

And when we walk in His love and yield to and obey the Spirit of Christ within us, we will always love and forgive one another. And we will know for sure that He abides within us by the same Spirit that He has already given all true believers.

"And he that keepeth his commandments dwelleth in him, and he in him. And hereby we know that he abideth in us, by the Spirit which he hath given us." (1 John 3: 24)

Although we are saved and justified by grace through faith and not by our own works, we have also been "created in Christ Jesus unto good works." But these are the works that the Spirit inspires in us so we can expect to be very strongly motivated to do them for God has ordained for us to "walk in them."

"For by grace are ye saved through faith; and that not of yourselves: it is the gift of God: Not of works, lest any man should boast. For we are his workmanship, created in Christ Jesus unto good works, which God hath before ordained that we should walk in them." (Ephesians 2: 8-10)

# Part III

---

# The Root of Bitterness

*How Bitterness Takes Root*

We are all spirit beings who have a soul (which is our mind, will, and emotions), and we all live in physical bodies. The human spirit that we inherited from our ancestors has been defiled both by their sins and by our own sins, so that is why we all need a Savior and a new birth.

"May God himself, the God of peace, sanctify you through and through. May your whole spirit, soul and body be kept blameless at the coming of our Lord Jesus Christ" (I Thessalonians 5: 23 NIV)

And the Spirit of God is obviously already blameless, so the apostle Paul must be referring to our human spirit that we inherited from our ancestors and not to the Holy Spirit which comes directly from the Father.

Even after our human spirit has been cleansed by the "new birth" we can still sin, so that is why "your whole spirit, soul and body" needs to be kept blameless by confession and sincere repentance in accordance with the following scripture.

"If we say that we have no sin, we deceive ourselves, and the truth is not in us. If we confess our sins, he is faithful and just to forgive us our sins, and to cleanse us from all unrighteousness." (I John 1: 8-9)

If various negative emotions like unforgiveness have not been confessed and repented while they are still in the early stages, they could eventually turn into a much more serious root of bitterness.

We all grieve after a loss but not everyone will become bitter. A root of bitterness usually begins after a loss when people start blaming either God or someone else for their own misfortune in order to justify their own selves.

First, there is always a loss.

There is always some kind of a loss before a root of bitterness can begin to grow. For Cain it was the loss of his favor with God. For Job it was the loss of his family, his wealth, and his health. For you it could be any number of things, such as the loss of your reputation, finances, security, marital love, family relationships, self-esteem, etc.

Second, there is always blame.

If you really do have a root of bitterness, you will find yourself wanting to blame someone else for your own problems or misfortune.

You might blame God, your spouse, your parents, your lawyer, your government, or maybe even your friends who are trying to help you. And if you are unable to blame anyone or anything else, then you may even blame yourself for "being so stupid! "

However, the latter is only a subtle form of pride, for no one is perfect, and we all make mistakes. As a matter of fact, that is why we all need Jesus. And if you really do have a root of bitterness, you may not like to hear this, but I would like you to get "better" and not "bitter" so I will tell you anyway.

I believe that the root cause of bitterness is really a self-righteous spirit that rejects the grace and the love of God and then seeks to be justified by blaming others for their own faults or shortcomings.

This truth may be hard to receive at first, but you can take consolation in the fact that we all struggle at times with our pride, ego, and self-righteousness.

And instead of admitting our own faults, we all have a tendency to blame others for our own mistakes.

Eve did it by blaming the serpent!

Adam did it by blaming Eve!

Cain did it by blaming Abel!

Job did it by blaming God!

Saul did it by blaming the People!

At this point, it is time for you to honestly search your own heart to see if this applies to you. Have you been trying to justify your own failings or misfortune by blaming others?

The other person may even be mostly at fault, but before you pronounce judgment, Jesus taught that you should "first cast the beam out of thine own eye, and then thou shalt see dearly to cast the mote [a small speck] out of thy brother's eye."

"And why beholdest thou the mote that is in thy brother's eye, but perceivest not the beam that is in thine own eye? Either how canst thou say to thy brother, Brother, let me pull out the mote that is in thine eye, when thou thyself beholdest not the beam that is in thine own eye? Thou hypocrite, cast out first the beam out of thine own eye, and then shalt thou see clearly to pull out the mote that is in thy brother's eye. " (Luke 6: 41-42)

As indicated, even if you only have a very small speck of "faults" in your own eye, you will still have to confess your own faults if you want to see clearly to help correct someone else. And if you should have to correct someone, it must still be done very humbly "In a spirit of meekness" out of pure love for that person and never out of anger, wrath, or rage!

"Brethren, if a man be overtaken in a fault, ye which are spiritual, restore such a one in the spirit of meekness; considering thyself, lest thou also be tempted." (Galatians 6: 1)

Self-righteous and egotistic people do not want to change or admit any weaknesses, so they will often try to justify themselves by blaming others. Humble people will readily admit their own failings, so they are quick to apologize for their part. And in some cases, they may even offer to make restitution for any harm that may have occurred.

"What is more, I consider everything a loss because of the surpassing worth of knowing Christ Jesus my Lord, for whose sake I have lost all things. I consider them garbage, that I may gain Christ and be found in him, not having a righteousness of my own that comes from the law, but that which is through faith in Christ." (Romans 3: 8-9 NIV)

## The Consequences of Bitterness

A "root of bitterness" must have been very common in Bible days, for the following scripture says that "many" were defiled by it. And if we should "fail of the face of God", then a "root of bitterness" could also spring up within us as well.

"Follow peace with all men, and holiness, without which no man shall see the Lord: Looking diligently you will still have to confess your own faults if you want to see clearly lest any man fail of the grace of God; lest any root of bitterness springing up to trouble you, and thereby many be defiled; Lest there be any fornicator, or profane person, as Esau, who for one morsel of meat sold his birthright." (Hebrews 12: 14-16)

The original Greek word for "bitterness" is "pikria" and is defined as "wickedness or hatred which has a bitter root that produces bitter fruit." And the way given to avoid producing "bitter fruit" is to "follow peace with all men, and holiness, without which no man shall see the Lord."

Sometimes people will say that they just don't want to forgive or be reconciled with someone, and you may also feel the same way. There are others who would really like to forgive someone so that they can "forget about it" but have been unable to do this for any attempts always end up in futile arguments.

If this has happened to you, then you may have developed a "root of bitterness." After in depth counseling, many discover that the real reason for their bitterness was an accumulation of past offenses that had never been completely forgiven.

Of course, there are various other negative emotions such as unjust anger, grudges, resentment, contempt, hatred, wickedness, jealousy, wrath, envy, (etc.) which could also develop into a "root of bitterness" if they are not resolved and forgiven.

Therefore if any of these other negative emotions should rise up whenever you think about or talk about a certain person or incident, or if you feel your mouth drop or your face stiffen whenever you think about or talk about that person or incident, then you have also most likely developed a "root of bitterness".

Cain is probably the best example of someone who let his disappointment develop into a "root of bitterness". When his brother Abel's offering was found to be very pleasing to God, and his own offering was rejected, Cain became very angry and his face (countenance) fell.

"And Abel, he also brought of the firstlings of his flock and of the fat thereof. And the Lord had respect unto Abel and to his offering: But unto Cain and to his offering he had not respect. And Cain was very wroth, and his countenance fell. And the Lord said unto Cain, why art thou wroth? and why is thy countenance fallen? If thou doest well, shalt thou not be accepted? And if thou doest not well, sin lieth at the door. And unto thee shall be his desire, and thou shalt rule over him." (Genesis 4: 4-7)

But Cain refused to let go of his anger and instead blamed his more righteous brother for his own inability to please God. As soon as he tried to justify himself by blaming his brother, a "root of bitterness" began to grow in his heart. This root grew larger until it eventually caused him to fulfill his irrational desires for revenge by murdering his own brother!

So the moral of this Bible story is this:

- Negative emotions like unforgiveness can turn into a root of bitterness.
- A root of bitterness begins with re-jecting the grace of God and then by blaming others falsely for the person's own misfortune.
- A root of bitterness can then lead into an overwhelming desire to get revenge.
- Violence, arguments, destruction of property, terrorism, and even murder can all be the result of prolonged and unresolved bitterness.

If a person should blame himself, then any desire for revenge will be turned inward. This can cause extreme depression, recklessness, self-hate, and even thoughts of suicide. And if a person should blame God, then the desire for revenge is expressed according to whether or not the person fears God.

When a person does not fear God, the desire for revenge is often expressed by blas-pheming God, practicing witchcraft, or by unrestrained wickedness.

### Job's Blamelessness

When a person fears God, the desire for revenge is suppressed, so the anger turns inward and causes extreme depression and feelings of despair and hopelessness.

The latter was the case with Job.

When major troubles came after he had tried so hard to please God, he first suppressed his anger and tried not to blame God. But as his troubles increased even to the loss of his wealth, family, and health, he eventually did blame God and then became severely depressed.

Like Job's three friends, many Bible teachers present poor Job as being so "self- righteous" or "fearful" that he really deserved the calamities that came upon him.

This is like saying the apostle Paul, who preached God's love and abundant grace, deserved the beatings and the afflictions that he had to endure!

The truth is that both of these men were being tested and matured by making them more dependent upon God, so that he could bring them to an even higher level of faith which is "more precious than of gold."

"That the trial of your faith, being much more precious than of gold that perisheth, though it be tried with fire, might be found unto praise and honor and glory at the appearing of Jesus Christ." (1 Peter 1: 7)

The fact that Job was already blameless and loyal before he was afflicted was con-firmed in the very first paragraph, which says that "This man was blameless and upright; he feared God and shunned evil."

"In the land of Uz there lived a man whose name was Job. This man was blameless and upright; he feared God and shunned evil. He had seven sons and three daughters, and he owned seven thousand sheep, three thousand camels, five hundred yoke of oxen and five hundred donkeys, and had a large number of servants. He was the greatest man among all the people of the East." (Job 1: 1-3 NIV)

And knowing how Satan would react, God had "set him up" to test and purify Job's love when he was no longer blessed with abundant possessions. Satan, as the "accuser of the brethren", thought that Job would curse God when he lost his family and all of his possessions, but Job still remained faithful and continued to love and worship God.

"And said, 'Naked came I out of my mother's womb, and naked shall I return thither: the Lord gave, and the Lord hath taken away; blessed be the name of the Lord.' In all this Job sinned not, nor charged God foolishly." (Job 1: 21-22)

And when he became covered with very painful boils from head to toe, and when even his own wife said that he should "Curse God and die", he still remained faithful and did not sin with his words.

"His wife said to him, 'Are you still maintaining your integrity? Curse God and die!' He replied, 'You are talking like a foolish woman. Shall we accept good from God, and not trouble?' In all this, Job did not sin in what he said." (Job 2: 9-10 NIV)

But when Job's three friends came to try to "console" him with accusations, he began to question God. And when his friends mourned and wept aloud out of pity for him, this just made him feel even worse. And his grief was then so great that no one dared to speak a word to him for seven days.

"When they saw him from a distance, they could hardly recognize him; they began to weep aloud, and they tore their robes and sprinkled dust on their heads. Then they sat on the ground with him for seven days and seven nights. No one said a word to him, because they saw how great his suffering was. (Job 2: 12-13 NIV)

Although he still did not curse God as Satan had hoped, his hidden anger erupted from his depression, and he began to curse *himself* for being born. Then his own words caused him to turn back into a severe depression, for he knew that he could not do anything about it except to blame God for being unjust.

His three friends were no help at all and continued to give him very bad advice which only reaped even more condemnation upon him. But Job believed that the severity of his calamities were really not justified, so he very presumptuously asked for an audience with God so that they could debate the issue.

When God eventually did answer Job's request, He first revealed how little Job knew about everything in His creation, and then He rebuked Job for speaking so presumptuously. And when Job apologized, He went straight to the heart of the matter, which was that Job was really trying to justify himself by blaming God.

"Wilt thou condemn me, that *thou* may be justified?" (Job 40: 8)

Yes, Job did eventually blame God in order to justify himself, but he also had no knowledge at that time about Satan's evil involvement or even of God's great love for him. And he certainly did not know that God had allowed Satan to test him in order to strengthen Job's character, for he had pre-viously admitted that he "greatly feared" this might happen.

"For the thing which I greatly feared is come upon me, and that which I was afraid of is come unto me." (Job 3: 25)

And the reason that Job had "greatly feared" that this might happen is that he believed his prosperity was dependent upon his own works, and not upon God's mercy and love for him. *Fear is a form of unbelief*, for it denies the fact that "Every good and perfect gift is from above" and that God always has good motives.

"Don 't be deceived, my dear brothers and sisters. Every good and perfect gift is from above, coming down from the Father of the heavenly lights, who does not change like shifting shadows. He chose to give us birth through the word of truth, that we might be a kind of first fruits of all he created." (James 1: 16-18 NIV)

And although we all have free will, and He sometimes allows evil to come upon us, He still promises to work good out of every situation (Romans 8:28), for His thoughts and ways are much greater than our own thoughts and ways.

"For my thoughts are not your thoughts, neither are your ways my ways, saith the Lord. For as the heavens are higher than the earth, so are my ways higher than your ways, and my thoughts than your thoughts." (Isaiah 55: 8-9)

Although Job did eventually succumb to a root of bitterness by blaming God, he never denied his faith in God. And I don't think that you or I would do any better if we also suffered from so many calamities…

And Job's three "friends" (and maybe your own friends would do this too) only added to his suffering. This is because they were convinced that Job deserved these calamities, that he must have done and hidden some very big sins in order to have caused them.

The book of Job is believed to be the oldest book in the Bible, when little was known about the love and the righteous ways of our God. The book was written long before the Mosaic Laws were given, so Job and his friends knew nothing about God's great love for them and His future long term plans to redeem all mankind by sending His only begotten Son.

Was Job a little self-righteous? Yes, of course, but we all have at least some pride and self-righteousness in us, and we have all sinned. But Job's three friends were far more self-righteous, for they had falsely accused him of having done some very great sins and then had heaped "tons" of condemnation upon him.

And yet, in spite of the severe calamities that came upon him, Job still openly declared his faith in God, and that he knew that his redeemer not only lives, but that he would one day see him face to face.

"For I know that my redeemer liveth, and that he shall stand at the latter day upon the earth: And though after my skin worms destroy this body, yet in my flesh shall I see God: Whom I shall see for myself, and mine eyes shall behold, and not another; though my reins be consumed within me." (Job 19: 25-27)

When God did finally appear, He said that He was very angry with Job's three friends for they had not "spoken the truth about me, as my servant Job has." He then asked "his servant Job" to pray and intercede for his three friends so that He would not have to deal with them harshly for not speaking the truth.

Fortunately for Job's three friends, they quickly repented and did exactly what they were told, and the intercessory prayers of Job were then accepted by God as being sufficient to spare them from the consequences of their folly.

"After the LORD had said these things to Job, he said to Eliphaz the Temanite, "I am angry with you and your two friends, because you have not spoken the truth about me, as my servant Job has. So now take seven bulls and seven rams and go to my servant Job and sacrifice a burnt offering for yourselves. My servant Job will pray for you and I will accept his prayer and not deal with you according to your folly. You have not spoken the truth about me, as my servant Job has." So Eliphaz the Temanite, Bildad the Shuhite and Zophar the Naamathite did what the LORD told them; and the LORD accepted Job 's prayer." (Job 42: 7-9 NIV)

Not only did God honor Job by asking him to intercede for his three friends, but the prophet Ezekiel later revealed that Job was linked equally with two other spiritual giants, Noah and Daniel, whose prayers were also held in very high esteem by God.

"Son of man, if a country sins against me by being unfaithful and I stretch out my hand against it to cut off its food supply and send famine upon it and kill its people and their animals, even if these three men — Noah, Daniel and Job — were in it, they could save only themselves by their righteousness, declares the Sovereign LORD." (Ezekiel 14: 13-14 NIV)

Although their gifts and their callings were quite different, all of these three spiritual giants were obedient and faithful to their callings, for they had continued to serve God in spite of many severe trials and extremely difficult circumstances.

God never did really explain to Job why He had permitted (and even had "set up") Satan to do so much evil against Job, but I believe that the main reason was to humble and mature Job with adversity, like He also did later with the apostle Paul. And if this was His goal, then it appears to have worked very well for Job was never heard to complain again.

If you should feel that your own life has been very similar to Job's life, then I have some really good news that should greatly encourage you:

After Job was greatly humbled and made more mature by his adversities; he was then given twice as much material wealth as he had before and his seven sons and three daughters whom he had lost were even replaced with his new seven new sons and three new daughters.

And Job's own life was extended for one hundred and forty additional years so that he could enjoy his restored prosperity and honor along with his children, his grand-children, and his great grandchildren, and even their children unto the fourth generation.

Note: He was probably also blessed with a new and a much better wife as 20 children would most likely have been too much for a single woman to bear.

So if your life has really been like Job's life, then after you have been made more mature through your overcoming adversity, something like this could also happen to you, for God is not a respecter of persons.

"The LORD blessed the latter part of Job 's life more than the former part. He had fourteen thousand sheep, six thousand camels, a thousand yoke of oxen and a thousand donkeys. And he also had seven sons and three daughters. The first daughter he named Jemimah, the second Keziah and the third Keren-Happuch. Nowhere in all the land were there found women as beautiful as Job 's daughters, and their father granted them an inheritance along with their brothers. After this, Job lived a hundred and forty years; he saw his children and their children to the fourth generation." (Job 42: 12-16 NIV)

## Freedom from Bitterness

Job apologized and became free from a root of bitterness after God appeared and rebuked him. But it is not likely that God will appear to you in the same way, so you should now ask Him to help you get free from your own root of bitterness. One of the signs of humility is to admit your own weaknesses and then to seek help from God and from others.

The following are seven additional steps that you can take that should help you become free from a root of bitterness so that you can enjoy your life once again.

### 1. Stop Blaming Others

"But if ye have bitter envying and strife in your hearts, glory not, and lie not against the truth. This wisdom descendeth not from above, but is earthly, sensual, devilish. For where envying and strife is, there is confusion and every evil work." (James 3: 14-16)

The first thing you should do is immediately stop blaming others, even if most of the fault should be what the others had done. Don't forget that you are only re-sponsible for your own faults, and you are not responsible for the faults or shortcomings of others, so stop blaming them and look into your own heart and correct whatever needs to change.

You can stop blaming others im-mediately as an act of your free will, and this does not require any repentance or change in your attitude. However, to be completely free, you will eventually have to repent and change your attitude so that you can forgive everyone, including yourself for your own mistakes.

As stated previously, there is always some kind of a loss before a root of bitterness can begin to grow. For Cain it was the loss of his favor with God. For Job it was the loss of his family, his wealth, and his health. For you it could be any number of things, such as the loss of your reputation, finances, security, marital love, family relationships, self-esteem, etc.

And since a root of bitterness usually includes the rejecting of the grace of God, and then trying to be justified by blaming someone else, you most likely already have a root        of bitterness if you are continuing to blame someone else for your own misfortune.

And maybe you have been going down the road of bitterness for a very long time and you have already progressed from only lightly blaming others to now having major anger problems that also include an overwhelming desire to get revenge.

If you should blame yourself, then any desire for revenge will turn inward. This can result in extreme depression, recklessness, self-hate, and maybe even thoughts of suicide. And if you should blame God, then the revenge would be expressed according to whether or not you fear God.

When a person does not fear God, the desire for revenge may be expressed by blaspheming the name of God, practicing witchcraft, or by unrestrained wickedness and evil. But if a person does fear God, then the desire for revenge will be suppressed, so the anger turns inward and causes severe depression and feelings of despair and hopelessness.

The latter was the case with Job. When troubles came, he first suppressed his anger and tried not to blame God. But as his troubles increased, he eventually did blame God. And then he became very depressed and frustrated when he realized that he couldn't do anything about it except complain.

What was God's response?

First, He rebuked Job for speaking so presumptuously. Then He went straight to the heart of the matter, which was that Job was really frying to justify himself by blaming God!

"Wilt thou condemn me, that *thou* may be justified?" (Job 40:8)

So if you are still very angry and thinking of different ways to "get even" with someone, I don't think that you have to be reminded that you should immediately stop any further action in this direction.

"Those who guard their mouths and their tongues keep themselves from calamity." (Proverbs 21:23 NIV)

And if you still do not want to repent and stop blaming others, you should be warned that even for Christian believers, there is no sacrifice available for deliberate and willful sins once you have learned the truth. So if you should continue in this direction, the severe judgment of God will surely follow.

"For if we sin willfully after we have received the knowledge of the truth, there remaineth no more sacrifice for sins, but a certain fearful looking for of judgment and fiery indignation, which shall devour the adversaries." (Hebrews 10: 26-27)

We are all imperfect and we all sin, but we do not all continue to do the same sins "after we have received the knowledge of the truth." Nevertheless, like the father who loved his prodigal son, God will still welcome us back if we will repent and return to Him.

"Get rid of all bitterness, rage and anger, brawling and slander, along with every form of malice. Be kind and compassionate to one another, forgiving each other, just as in Christ God forgave you." (Ephesians 4: 31-32 NIV)

## 2. Humble Yourself and Pray

Since the root cause of bitterness is apparently self-righteousness, the next major thing you should do is to humble yourself and pray, seek the Lord, and turn away from any wicked ways.

"If my people, which are called by my name, shall humble themselves, and pray, and seek my face, and turn from their wicked ways; then will I hear from heaven, and will forgive their sin, and will heal their land." (2 Chronicles 7: 14)

You can begin by confessing your own sins and weaknesses so that God can forgive you and cleanse you from all unrighteousness. And if you are able to do so at this time, you should also pray for those you have found to be difficult to forgive.

No man is an island, and we all need God and each other. One of the symptoms of self-righteousness is to think that we do not need any help from anyone else even if it should be from our own Creator.

Humility is simply believing the ab-solute truth about ourselves from God's perspective and relying upon our God who made the whole universe. In other words, we should always think of ourselves as being neither higher nor lower than what we really are.

"Humble yourselves therefore under the mighty hand of God, that he may exalt you in due time: Casting all your care upon him; for he careth for you." (1 Peter 5: 6-7)

Probably the best way to humble yourself is to begin with the very basic truth that "all have sinned and come short of the glory of God." This in itself is very humbling for it requires that everyone must depend upon a Savior to rescue us from our own weaknesses.

"For all have sinned, and come short of the glory of God; Being justified freely by his grace through the redemption that is in Christ Jesus:" (Romans 3: 23-24)

Even belittling ourselves with self-deprecating humor can be false humility if it hides the subtle hope of being exalted. And humility can be a most elusive thing for we all have at least some prides for as it is writ-        ten, "There is none righteous, no, not one." (Romans 3:10)

So what are we to do?

Jesus gave us the answer on how to be humble, for He is the only person in the world who can honestly say that He was "humble in heart." That is why He wants us to take His "yoke" upon us and to learn from Him.

"Come to me, all you who are weary and burdened, and I will give you rest. Take my yoke upon you and learn from me, for I am gentle and humble in heart, and you will find rest for your souls." (Matthew 11: 28-29 NIV)

Jesus ministered to many sinners, but the only ones He really spoke harshly to were the religious leaders who were filled with pride and self-righteousness. Ministry or business leaders are especially vulnerable to the sin of pride because they tend to become puffed up by the adulation of their followers.

And even God-ordained leaders can start out like King Saul, by being humble and "little in their own eyes" and then end up losing their humility and their ministry, employment, or business.

Over the years, I have seen many very prominent Christian leaders, and even some godly lay people, sin and fall from the grace of God when their very own success caused them to lose their humility.

There is a similar principle in the business world called "The Peter Principle." (No relation to the apostle) This tongue in cheek theory was first introduced by Dr. Laurence J. Peter and Raymond Hull in a book of the same name. The "Peter Principle" is about those who are promoted higher and higher until they reach their own "level of incompetence".

This can also happen to Christian leaders as well. The apostle Peter provided the following wise advice for church Pastors and others who have been entrusted with high positions of leadership and responsibility. He urged them to humbly serve others and not to "lord it over" those entrusted to their care.

"Be shepherds of God's flock that is under your care, serving as overseers - not because you must, but because you are willing, as God wants you to be; not greedy for money, but eager to serve; not lording it over those entrusted to you, but being examples to the flock. And when the Chief Shepherd appears, you will receive the crown of glory that will never fade away " (1 Peter 5: 2-4 NIV)

The apostle Peter also gave wise advice for the young people who will become our future leaders. He reminded them to "clothe themselves with humility" and to always be submissive and respectful to those who are older, for God resists the proud and gives his grace only to those who are humble.

"Young men, in the same way be submissive to those who are older. All of you, clothe yourselves with humility toward one another, because God opposes the proud but gives grace to the humble. Humble yourselves, therefore, under God's mighty hand, that he may lift you up in due time." (1 Peter 5: 5-6 NIV)

### 3. Confess Your Own Faults.

The next thing that you should do to overcome a root of bitterness is to acknowledge and confess your own sins and faults, and not the sins or faults of others. When you admit or "confess" your sins and faults to God, He will cleanse you from all unrighteousness so that you can see more clearly and stop judging or talking negatively about any other person.

"If we say that we have no sin, we deceive ourselves, and the truth is not in us. If we confess our sins, he is faithful and just to forgive us our sins, and to cleanse us from all unrighteousness." (I John 1: 8-9)

In the Alcoholics Anonymous pro-grams, they often urge its members to take their own "inventory" (faults or sins) and never to take another person's "inventory' (faults or sins).

This same principle is also revealed very clearly in the parable of the Pharisee and the publican. The Pharisee was only self-righteously exalting himself when he prayed, but the humble publican (tax collector) did not blame anyone else and only confessed his own sins while earnestly seeking God's love, mercy, grace, and forgiveness.

"The Pharisee stood and prayed thus with himself, God, I thank thee, that I am not as other men are, extortioners, unjust, adulterers, or even as this publican. I fast twice in the week; I give tithes of all that I possess. And the publican, standing afar off, would not lift up so much as his eyes unto heaven, but smote upon his breast, saying, God be merciful to me a sinner. I tell you, this man went down to his house justified rather than the other: for every one that exalteth himself shall be abased; and he that humbleth himself shall be exalted." (Luke 18: 11-14)

Even if the major portion of the fault may be with the other person and you only have a much smaller portion of the fault, you should still only confess your own sins and leave the judgment of the other person up to God who always judges righteously.

"Do not judge or you too will be judged. For in the same way you judge others, you will be judged, and with the measure you use, it will be measured to you. "Why do you look at the speck of sawdust in your brother 's eye and pay no attention to the plank in your own eye? How can you say to your brother, 'Let me take the speck out of your eye, ' when all the time there is a plank in your own eye? You hypocrite, first take the plank out of your own eye, and then you will see clearly to remove the speck from your brother 's eye. (Matthew 7: 1-5 NIV)

When you are in a group of trustworthy Christians, it is also very liberating and cleans-ing to be able to share your faults and shortcomings with them so that they can pray for you. However, you should be very careful as to how much you share, for much damage can be done even by "born again" but unsanctified Christians who may be more in the flesh than in the Spirit. (Romans 8:5-8)

"Confess your faults one to another, and pray one for another, that ye may be healed. The effectual fervent prayer of a righteous man availeth much. Elias was a man subject to like passions as we are, and he prayed earnestly that it might not rain: and it rained not on the earth by the space of three years and six months. And he prayed again, and the heaven gave rain, and the earth brought forth her fruit." (James 5: 16-18)

### 4. Speak Only Blessings

Speak only blessings and good things and don't be critical of others. This may be difficult to do at first for being excessively critical may have now become habitual and hard to stop.

"Out of the same mouth proceedeth blessing and cursing. My brethren, these things ought not so to be." (James 3: 10)

It is written that death and life are in the power of the tongue (Proverbs 18:21), for spoken words can either build people up or they can tear people down. You cannot always control your thoughts, but you can certainly control what you speak.

"The tongue of the just is as choice silver: the heart of the wicked is little worth. The lips of the righteous feed many: but fools die for want of wisdom. The blessing of the Lord, it maketh rich, and he addeth no sorrow with it." (Proverbs 10: 20-22)

If you speak kind and positive words, then people will be blessed; but if you speak negative words, your words will be the same as a curse to all who receive them. The tongue is a very small member in the body, but it can corrupt and defile the whole body.

When we put bits into the mouths of horses to make them obey us, we can turn the whole animal. Or take ships as an example. Although they are so large and are driven by strong winds, they are steered by a very small rudder wherever the pilot wants to go.

Likewise, the tongue is a small part of the body, but it makes great boasts. Consider how a great forest is set on fire by a small spark.

"The tongue also is a fire, a world of evil among the parts of the body. It corrupts the whole body, sets the whole course of one 's life on fire, and is itself set on fire by hell." (James 3: 3-6 NIV)

When God created the universe, He spoke it into existence, and His Holy Spirit manifested it. And since we were created in His image, we too must "speak" what we believe. The late Kenneth E. Hagin once said that the problem with most Christians is not so much in their believing but in their not "speaking" what they want to believe.

"'Have faith in God', Jesus answered. 'Truly I tell you, if anyone says to this mountain, Go, throw yourself into the sea, and does not doubt in their heart but believes that what they say will happen, it will be done for them." (Mark 11: 22-23 NIV)

When God wanted to bless Israel, He had Moses tell Aaron (his spokesman) to "speak" to the nation the following priestly blessing. God's blessing was then imparted by Aaron by his "speaking" it to the nation.

"And the LORD spake unto Moses, saying, Speak unto Aaron and unto his sons, saying, On this wise ye shall bless the children of Israel, saying unto them, The LORD bless thee, and keep thee: The LORD make his face shine upon thee, and be gracious unto thee: The

LORD lift up his countenance upon thee, and give thee peace. And they shall put my name upon the children of Israel, and I will bless them." (Numbers 6: 22-27)

The words that were spoken in the blessing also emphasized that God Himself was the source of that blessing, for "every good and perfect gift" must come directly from Him.

"Every good gift and every perfect gift is from above, and cometh down from the Father of lights, with whom is no variableness, neither shadow of turning." (James 1: 17)

As descendants of the first Adam, and by adoption the descendants of the second Adam (Jesus Christ), we were created to love God and one another and to "speak" only blessings and not curses to each other.

This is why we should always be careful to "let no corrupt communication proceed out of our mouths", and be willing to love and forgive one another even as God for Christ's sake has forgiven us.

"Let no corrupt communication proceed out of your mouth, but that which is good to the use of edifying, that it may minister grace unto the hearers. And grieve not the Holy Spirit of God, whereby ye are sealed unto the day of redemption. Let all bitterness, and wrath, and anger, and clamor, and evil speaking, be put away from you, with all malice: And be ye kind one to another, tenderhearted, forgiving one another, even as God for Christ's sake hath forgiven you." (Ephesians 4: 29-32)

So even if some people have done you great harm in the past, you should still be kind to them and only speak and do good things. And when you do good even to those who may hate you, "your reward will be great, and you will be children of the Most High, because he is kind to the ungrateful and wicked." (2 Corinthians 5:35 NIV)

"A good man out of the good treasure of the heart bringeth forth good things: and an evil man out of the evil treasure bringeth forth evil things. But I say unto you, that every idle word that men shall speak, they shall give account thereof in the Day of Judgment. For by thy words thou shalt be justified, and by thy words thou shalt be condemned." (Matthew 12: 35-37)


5.  Welcome Adversity

The title of this section may have shocked you as most people pray to avoid adversity, and they certainly do not welcome it. But "we know that all things work together for good to them that love God" and there are some spiritual values that can only be gained through adversity.

"And we know that all things work together for good to them that love God, to them who are the called according to his purpose. For whom he did foreknow, he also did predestinate to be conformed to the image of his Son, that he might be the firstborn among many brethren." (Romans 8: 28-29)

Even the great apostle Paul acknowledged that he was humbled with adversity in order to keep him from being prideful. He said that he had been given so many supernatural revelations that the Lord allowed a "messenger of Satan" to buffet him with a "thorn in the flesh" just to make sure that he did not succumb to the devastating sin of pride.

"To keep me from becoming conceited because of these surpassingly great revelations, there was given me a thorn in my flesh, a messenger of Satan, to torment me. Three times I pleaded with the Lord to take it away from me. But he said to me, 'My grace is sufficient for you, for my power is made perfect in weakness.'" (2 Corinthians 12: 7-9 NIV)

Paul prayed three times for relief, but he stopped abruptly when the Lord revealed that His grace was sufficient and that His miracle working power would only operate through humble vessels. Then Paul went to the other extreme and he even began to glory in his own weaknesses, insults, hardships, persecutions, and difficulties.

"Therefore I will boast all the more gladly about my weaknesses, so that Christ's power may rest on me. That is why, for Christ's sake, I delight in weaknesses, in insults, in hardships, in persecutions, in difficulties. For when I am weak, then I am strong." (2 Corinthians 12: 9-10 NIV)

And when the apostle Paul understood that his weaknesses made him even more dependent upon the anointing and the power of Almighty God, he then preached that "when I am weak, then I am strong."

So we can always be joyful.

"Blessed are you when people insult you, persecute you and falsely say all kinds of evil against you because of me. Rejoice and be glad, because great is your reward in heaven, for in the same way they persecuted the prophets who were before you." (Matthew 5: 11-12 NIV)

The apostle James also confirmed that we should count it all joy when we have adversity, for he also realized that trials and tastings, when received properly, will increase our faith and make us "mature and complete" and thus more like Jesus.

"Consider it pure joy, my brothers and sisters, whenever you face trials of many kinds, because you know that the testing of your faith produces perseverance. Let perseverance finish its work so that you may be mature and complete, not lacking anything." (James 1: 2-4 NIV)

And the apostle Peter also confirmed that we should "greatly rejoice" when we suffer all kinds of trials, for they prove the genuine-ness of our faith, and this is far more precious than even gold.

"In all this you greatly rejoice, though now for a little while you may have had to suffer grief in all kinds of trials. These have come so that the proven genuineness of your faith —of greater worth than gold, which perishes even though refined by fire — may result in praise, glory and honor when Jesus Christ is revealed." (1 Peter: 6-7 NIV)

And, of course, there is also the example of Jesus Christ Himself "who for the joy that was set before him endured the cross."

"Wherefore seeing we also are compassed about with so great a cloud of witnesses, let us lay aside every weight, and the sin which doth so easily beset us, and let us run with patience the race that is set before us, Looking unto Jesus the author and finisher of our faith; who for the joy that was set before him endured the cross, despising the shame, and is set down at the right hand of the throne of God." (Hebrews 12: 1-2)

And don't forget that our life on this earth is only temporary. When Jesus returns to give out His rewards (Revelation 22: 12), I suspect that some will rejoice greatly, but that some will be greatly disappointed and wished that they had done more when they realize what they could have had. To those in the church at Philadelphia who overcame ad-versity by patiently enduring their trials, Jesus said:

"Him that overcometh will I make a pillar in the temple of my God, and he shall go no more out; and I will write upon him the name of my God, and the name of the city of my God, the new Jerusalem, which cometh down from heaven from my God; and I will write upon him my new name." (Revelation 3: 12)

That is why the apostle Paul advises us all to "make it our goal to please Him (Jesus)" for we all must one day appear before the judgment seat of Christ to receive the rewards for what we have done while we were on the earth.

"We are confident, I say, and would prefer to be away from the body and at home with the Lord. So we make it our goal to please him, whether we are at home in the body or away from it. For we must all appear before the judgment seat of Christ, so that each of us may receive what is due us for the things done while in the body, whether good or bad." (2 Corinthians 5: 8-10 NIV)

## 6.  Be Thankful For What You Do Have

You cannot be bitter and grateful at the same time, so the next step in overcoming a root of bitterness is to have a heartfelt attitude of gratitude and thankfulness for the good-ness, mercy, and the grace of God that you have already received.

Even if you should still have lots of problems, you can still be very thankful and appreciative for the blessings that you already do have. Bad things still happen to good people, for we live in a hostile world, but we know that our God is able to use all of our life experiences, both the good and the bad, to help mature us and to make us more like His only begotten Son, Jesus Christ, our Lord.

My earthly father used to say that the man who had no shoes stopped complaining when he met the man with no feet. And no matter what else bad may happen, we can always be eternally grateful and thankful for our assurance of eternal life with our Lord and Savior, Jesus Christ.

And as our love relationship with our God grows and matures, we are then able to be joyful and pray continuously and "give thanks in all circumstances" even when we are being unjustly treated or persecuted.

"Make sure that nobody pays back wrong for wrong, but always try to be kind to each other and to everyone else. Be joyful always; pray continually; give thanks in all circumstances, for this is God's will for you in Christ Jesus." (1 Thessalonians 5: 15-18 NIV)

Gratitude is the seed for God to do even more for you. When we are thankful and appreciative, this opens up God's heart to bless us even more. But if we are ungrateful for what He has already given us, then we are like spoiled and bratty children. And when we are like that, why should He do more?

It is not wrong to seek God for more and more blessings, but we should also take the time once in awhile to look back and express our appreciation and praise for what He has already done for us.

"Let the peace of Christ rule in your hearts, since as members of one body you were called to peace. And be thankful. Let the message of Christ dwell among you richly as you teach and admonish one another with all wisdom through psalms, hymns, and songs from the Spirit, singing to God with gratitude in your hearts." (Colossians 3: 15-16 NIV)

Anger, anxiety, depression, bitterness, resentment, jealousy, and all of the other negative emotions cannot continue to exist in us when we are thankful and appreciative for all that God and His beloved Son have already done for us.

"Do not be anxious about anything, but in everything, by prayer and petition, with thanksgiving, present your requests to God. And the peace of God, which transcends all understanding, will guard your hearts and your minds in Christ Jesus." (Philippians 4: 6-7)

The "peace of God" is a supernatural peace that "transcends all understanding." Like the corresponding word for peace in the Hebrew (shalom), this kind of peace has the sense of complete rest, contentment, and wholeness.

### 7.  Love, Praise, and Worship God

The final step for deliverance from a root of bitterness is simply to love, praise, and wor-ship God. Our loving and praising Him for all He has done for us will renew our trust in Him and draw His presence closer, for He inhabits our praises (Psalm 22:3).

A good way to describe the progression of our relationship with God is that we first get to know Him when we are spiritually reborn and "enter into his gates with thanksgiving." Then we get to know Him better when we enter "into his courts with praise."

"Enter into his gates with thanksgiving, and into his courts with praise: be thankful unto him, and bless his name. For the Lord is good; his mercy is everlasting; and his truth endureth to all generations." (Psalm 100: 4-5)

True worship begins when we love Him with all of our heart, and this allows us to enter into His very holy presence as symbolized by the "Holy of Holies." This is also where God purifies our souls and sets us free from any root of bitterness as well as all other negative emotions.

"Jesus said, 'But the hour cometh and now is, when the true worshipers shall worship the Father in spirit and in truth; for the Father seeketh such to worship him.'" (John 4: 23)

Worship is our most intense love for God that we can have, and it is expressed mostly as an emotion. But whether it is in a loud voice or in reverent silence; whether it is in a church or at home; true worship is an intense love and adoration that comes from deep within our hearts and minds.

So if you will worship God sincerely "in spirit and in truth," you will then be able to spend time in His holy presence and partake of His divine nature. And it is in His presence where He replaces the negative emotions that had once caused us bitterness with His positive emotions of love, joy, and peace!

"For the kingdom of God is not meat and drink; but righteousness, and peace, and joy in the Holy Ghost." (Romans 14: 17)

After you have prayed for God's mercy and grace and stopped blaming others; humbled yourself by admitting your own faults; boldly confronted adversity as being redemptive; expressed gratitude for what you already do have; are speaking only the blessings of God, and have given thanks, praise, and all the Glory to God and our Lord and Savior Jesus Christ, you should no longer be suffering from a "root of bitterness."

And you should therefore find it very easy to forgive all who had once offended you. However, if you are still unable to feel a complete release of all feelings of unforgiveness right away, do not think you have failed. Forgiveness is often a process that begins as a decision and then becomes more complete with time.

Perhaps re-reading specific sections of this book may also be helpful. And just as there are degrees in the amount of love that you can have for another person, there can also be degrees in the amount of love and forgiveness.

### Corrie Ten Boom's Example

Corrie Ten Boom is an excellent example of how we can all learn to love and even be able to forgive our very worst enemies. When I first met her, we were both in Orleans Massachusetts attending a Christian teaching ministry led by two charismatic women, Cay Andersen, and Judy Sorenson.

Their teachings emphasized the im-portance of our complete  submission unto the will of God by "dying to self" and by yielding to the Spirit of God within us. (Romans 6: 13) This teaching was primarily based upon the following scripture.

"Verily, verily, I say unto you, except a corn of wheat fall into the ground and die, it abideth alone: but if it die, it bringeth forth much fruit. He that loveth his life shall lose it; and he that hateth his life in this world shall keep it unto life eternal." (John 12: 24-25)

Corrie was then well into her eighties and was already famous because of her bestselling autobiographical book, "The Hiding Place". I observed her listening very intently to the speaker and busily taking notes just so that she could learn even more about the Lord that she loved so much.

And I was also impressed with her genuine humility when I heard her humbly asking for prayer that the Lord would keep her from becoming prideful, for she knew that a movie was about to be coming out about her life.

When Peter and Edith Marshall were pastors of a church in West Dennis on Cape Cod, I also had another chance to meet with her again and to hear her preach from their pulpit.

I especially liked the part in her sermon where she had praised God even for the fleas. This was because the fleas kept the guards outside the barracks in her concentration camp so that the prisoners could continue to pray and have private Bible studies.

Although her own father and sister had died while in the Nazi prison camps because of the extreme cruelty of the camp guards and leaders, she was still able to preach that "There is no pit so deep, that God's love is not deeper still." After the service, others gave her a very polite handshake when they were introduced to her, but I gave her a big hug!

For those who don't know about Corrie Ten Boom, she was arrested and eventually put into the concentration camp at Ravensbruck, Germany, by the Nazis during the Second World War, along with her elderly father and older sister, for having hidden Jews in their home in Holland.

If they had not hidden them, the Jews would have faced certain imprisonment and almost certain death in what we now call the "Holocaust." The nation of Israel has since even honored her sacrifice in their behalf by planting a tree in her memory and declaring her to be "a righteous gentile."

She was released from the prison camp on December 30, 1944, simply because of a clerical error (which was really a miracle of God) only a week before other women her age group were being executed. She then had the opportunity to preach all over the world the message that "love is stronger than hate."

But Conie also had to confess her own struggle in learning how to love and forgive the prison guards who had showed no mercy to her or her family. As it is so often, it is a lot easier to preach about love and forgiveness than it is to practice it.

She was once preaching on the importance of forgiveness in Munich, Germany when she recognized a man who had been an SS prison guard in the processing center at Ravensbruck. He came up after the service to compliment her for her wonderful message on forgiveness. He said that he did not remember her, but that he was now a Christian and wanted to ask for her forgiveness.

Corrie relates in her book how angry thoughts and memories had immediately raced through her mind. She knew that she had to forgive him, but it was not easy. She had to pray silently for the Lord to help by giving her *His forgiveness*, for she knew that she could not do it alone.

When she did stoically forgive him as an act of obedience, she was surprised when the overwhelming love of God suddenly came upon her. Then she really did love this former Nazi guard whom her Lord had so gloriously forgiven and redeemed. She gave God all the glory, for she knew that it was really *His* forgiveness that had set her free, for it was beyond her own ability to forgive so much evil.

A full transcript of this very inspirational story of her ultimate forgiveness of the former Nazi guard who had done so much evil has been recorded in a separate article by Guideposts Magazine, and her entire life story may be found in her autobiographical book entitled, "The Hiding Place."

"By mercy and truth iniquity is purged: and by the fear of the Lord men depart from evil. When a man's ways please the Lord, he maketh even his enemies to be at peace with him." (Proverbs 16: 6-7)

## There is No Bitterness in Love

"If we love one another, God dwelleth in us, and his love is perfected in us. Hereby know we that we dwell in him, and he in us, because he hath given us of his Spirit. And we have seen and do testify that the Father sent the Son to be the Savior of the world.

Whosoever shall confess that Jesus is the Son of God, God dwelleth in him, and he in God. And we have known and believed the love that God hath to us. God is love; and he that dwelleth in love dwelleth in God, and God in him.

Herein is our love made perfect, that we may have boldness in the Day of Judgment: because as he is, so are we in this world." (1 John 4: 12-17)

The preceding scripture is an excellent summary of how God's love when it is perfected in us can remove all bitterness, and change us so completely that we would be able to say boldly in the Day of Judgment, "As he is, so are we in this world."

There is obviously no bitterness in God, so we know that there was no bitterness in His Son, even when He was being crucified. As a matter of fact, Jesus even had some joy in the midst of His intense pain, for He could see the divine purpose in His suffering. He was looking forward to the future forgiveness and eternal salvation of millions of believers.

No matter how bad the circumstances may be in your own life, if you will abide in the victorious Spirit of Christ and walk in His love and do not grieve the Holy Spirit, you can also have joy in your heart and be able to forgive all who have offended you.

"And grieve not the Holy Spirit of God, whereby ye are sealed unto the day of redemption. Let all bitterness, and wrath, and anger, and clamor, and evil speaking, be put away from you, with all malice: And be ye kind one to another, tenderhearted, forgiving one another, even as God for Christ's sake hath forgiven you." (Ephesians 4: 30-31)

Consider Deacon Stephen's example.

Even while Stephen was being brutally executed, he was still able to pray for God to forgive those who were stoning him to death, saying "Lord, lay not this sin to their charge!"

As far as we know, the deacon Stephen never had a problem with unforgiveness, so he had nothing to repent of before he died. But even if he did, he was certainly abiding in the love of God where there can be no bitterness.

This is why I consider both Stephen and Jesus as excellent examples of how we should pray and believe whenever a person refuses to repent and is continuing to torment, persecute, or do us harm.

"When the members of the Sanhedrin heard this, they were furious and gnashed their teeth at him. But Stephen, full of the Holy Spirit, looked up to heaven and saw the glory of God, and Jesus standing at the right hand of God. "Look, " he said, "I see heaven open and the Son of Man standing at the right hand of God."

At this they covered their ears and, yelling at the top of their voices; they all rushed at him, dragged him out of the city and began to stone him. Meanwhile, the witnesses laid their coats at the feet of a young man named Saul. While they were stoning him, Stephen prayed, "Lord Jesus, receive my spirit. " Then he fell on his knees and cried out, "Lord, do not hold this sin against them." When he had said this, he fell asleep." (Acts 7: 54-60 NIV)

Forgiving and praying for one another is also a healing process in itself that can heal both parties at the same time. So when Stephen prayed, "Lord, do not hold this sin against them", he became the "poster child" for those who want to know how to pray for those who stubbornly refuse to repent.

As I said earlier in this book, I thought about those in my own life who have not repented and yet still need forgiveness from God. I could not pray for them in the usual way, so I decided to pray in a way that was similar to how Stephen had so effectively prayed for those who were stoning him.

Many Bible scholars believe that it was most likely Stephen's prayer that was responsible for extending the grace of God unto the unbelieving Saul (who was later renamed Paul) so that he could be given a vision of Jesus and be converted to Christianity. (Acts 9: 17) At this particular time, Saul had little or no merit of his own, for he was still having many Christians executed, beaten, or put into prison for blasphemy.

Consider also our Lord's example.

Even as He was dying on the cross, Jesus was still able to pray for His heavenly Father to forgive all those who were crucifying Him, saying "Father, forgive them; for they know not what they do!" This was a very appropriate and merciful prayer as the Roman soldiers who were crucifying him were only carrying out orders from the governing au-thorities and rulers of Israel.

"When they came to the place called the Skull, they crucified him there, along with the criminals — one on his right, the other on his left. Jesus said, "Father, forgive them, for they do not know what they are doing." And they divided up his clothes by casting lots. (Luke 23: 33-34 NIV)

And even while Jesus was dying a very slow death and suffering for the sins of all mankind, Jesus was still able to express His love for the criminals who were also being crucified around Him.

One of the criminals even rebuked his fellow criminal for hurling insults at the totally innocent Jesus and acknowledged that they were just getting what they deserved. When Jesus was asked to remember him when He came into His Kingdom, He immediately responded by saying, "Truly I tell you, today you will be with me in paradise."

Now that was certainly a very generous reward for just saying a few words of belief about Jesus. But he had apparently repented of his prior crimes, so he was forgiven just like we were and was also given eternal life with our Lord and Savior Jesus Christ.

"One of the criminals who hung there hurled insults at him: "Aren 't you the Messiah? Save yourself and us!" But the other criminal rebuked him. "Don 't you fear God", he said, "since you are under the same sentence? We are punished justly, for we are getting what our deeds deserve. But this man has done nothing wrong." Then he said, "Jesus, remember me when you come into your kingdom." Jesus answered him, "Truly I tell you, today you will be with me in paradise." (Luke 23: 39-43 NIV)

## God is Preparing Us for Eternity

You will know for sure that the love of God has been fully perfected in you when you are able to "clothe yourself with compassion, kindness, humility, gentleness, and patience" and even pray for God to forgive those who had once caused you great harm. When you "put on" the pure and unselfish love of God, this is what will bind these virtues "all together in perfect unity."

"Therefore, as God's chosen people, holy and dearly loved, clothe yourselves with compassion, kindness, humility, gentleness and patience. Bear with each other and forgive one another if any of you has a grievance against someone. Forgive as the Lord forgave you. And over all these virtues put on love, which binds them all together in perfect unity." (Colossians 3: 12-14 NIV)

Man prepares for his own lifetime, but God prepares for eternity. And there is a spiritual hierarchy of sorts in His Kingdom, for some will be more mature than others. These are the ones who will be the most like Jesus, and who will thus have the highest positions of leadership in His eternal Kingdom.

"And Jesus said unto them, Verily I say unto you, That ye which have followed me, in the regeneration when the Son of Man shall sit in the throne of his glory, ye also shall sit upon twelve thrones, judging the twelve tribes of Israel." (Matthew 19: 28)

All true believers will live forever and wear the white "garment of salvation" for clothing, but some will also wear a "robe of righteousness" and even others will have a "crown of righteousness" upon their heads and big rewards. (Isaiah 61:10, 2 Timothy 4:8)

These will be the ones who will be more like Jesus and who will be our leaders during the millennium and afterwards in the new heavens and the new earth. They will rule with Jesus and radiate more of the light of His Glory throughout all eternity.

"Let not your heart be troubled: ye believe in God, believe also in me. In my Father's house are many mansions: if it were not so, I would have told you. I go to prepare a place for you. And if I go and prepare a place for you, I will come again, and receive you unto myself; that where I am, there ye may be also." (John 14: 1-3)

For those of us who have our names written in the Lamb's Book of Life, Jesus will give out our rewards when He returns according to our works while we were on this earth. So that is a very good reason why we should always "make it our goal to please him!"

"So we make it our goal to please him, whether we are at home in the body or away from it. For we must all appear before the judgment seat of Christ, so that each of us may receive what is due us for the things done while in the body, whether good or bad." (2 Corinthians 5: 9-10 NIV)

And you will be more likely to abide in His love and "walk in love, as Christ also hath loved us, "if you will voluntarily make it your own personal goal to be a true "follower of God."

"Be ye therefore followers of God, as dear children; and walk in love, as Christ also hath loved us, and hath given himself for us an offering and a sacrifice to God for a sweet smelling savor. But fornication, and all uncleanness, or covetousness, let it not be once named among you, as becometh saints." (Ephesians 5: 1-3)

Although we are all justified by the mercy and grace of God and faith in the finished work of our Lord Jesus Christ, we will still be rewarded for the works of God that we have done in obedience to His will while we are still on earth.

"And, behold, I come quickly; and my reward is with me, to give every man according as his work shall be. I am Alpha and Omega, the beginning and the end, the first and the last. Blessed are they that do his commandments, that they may have right to the tree of life and may enter in through the gates into the city." (Revelation 22: 12-14)

Now the question is, "What do you believe?" Do you believe Jesus is who He said He was? If you do, then do you want to receive Him now as your Savior and be "born again"? Although there is no set formula for being "born again", the following are four Scriptural steps to help you receive:

1.      Repent (turn away from willful sins)

2 Peter 3:9 "The Lord is not slack concerning His promise, as some men call slackness; but is longsuffering to usward, not willing that any should perish, but that all should come to repentance."

2.      Believe (believe that God's Son died for your sins)

Romans 5:6-9 "Christ died for the ungodly... but God commended His love toward us in that, while we were yet sinners, Christ died for us. Much more then, being justified [declared righteous] by His blood, we shall be saved from [God's] wrath through Him."

3.      Receive (receive Jesus as your own personal Savior)

John 1:12-13 "But as many as received Him [Jesus Christ], to them gave He power to become children of God, even to them who believe on His name; who were born, not of blood, nor of the will of the flesh, nor of the will of man, but of God."

4.      Confess (confess your faith in Jesus Christ to others)

Romans 10:9-13 "If thou shalt confess with thy mouth the Lord Jesus and believe in thine heart that God hath raised Him from the dead, thou shalt be saved."


If you are not sure whether or not you have really been "born again", just pray the following prayer or a similar prayer in your own words:

*Lord God, forgive me for my sins and cleanse me from all of my unrighteousness. I believe your Son Jesus Christ suffered and died on a cruel cross to pay the penalty for my sins.*

*Jesus, come into my heart and be the Lord of my life. With the help of your Holy Spirit, I want to live the rest of my life doing your perfect will.*

If your prayer was sincere, then your sins have now been forgiven, and the Spirit of Christ has come into your heart. (Galatians 4:6, John 14:23)

Although we are saved by grace through faith, and not by our own works, the Holy Spirit within you will now inspire you to do good works and live righteously.

Ephesians 2:8-10 "For by grace are ye saved through faith; and that not of yourselves, it is the gift of God. Not of works, lest any man should boast. For we are His workmanship, created in Christ Jesus unto good works, which God hath before ordained that we should walk in them."

The "religious" do good works out of fear to fry to gain God's favor.

We do good works out of love because we already have God's favor!

How do I know that I have been born again?

You will know this intuitively because the Holy Spirit will confirm to your human spirit that you are a child of God. But even if there are days when you don't feel like you have ever been "born again", you can always trust in God's Word, for "it is impossible for God to lie." (Hebrews 6:18)

The following Scriptures give assurance you have been "born again" and have eternal life:

1 Romans 8:15-16 "For ye have not received the spirit of bondage again to fear, but ye have received the spirit of adoption, whereby we cry, Abba, Father. The Spirit himself beareth witness with our [human] spirit, that we are the children of God."

John 5:10-13 "He that believeth on the Son of God hath the witness in himself ... He that hath the Son hath life; and he that hath not the Son hath not life. These things have I written unto you that believe on the name of the Son of God, that ye may know that ye have eternal life!"

John 3:37 "All that the Father giveth me [Jesus], shall come to me; and him that cometh to me [Jesus] I will in no wise cast out!"

John 10:27-30 "My sheep hear my voice, and I [Jesus] know them, and they follow me. And I [Jesus] give unto them eternal life; and they shall never perish, neither shall any man pluck them out of my hand. My Father, who gave them to me, is greater than all, and no man is able to pluck them out of my Father's hand, for I and my Father are one!"

I will leave you with a final blessing from my own heart:

*May the Lord bless you and keep you.*

*May the Lord make his face to shine upon you, and be gracious to you.*

*May the Lord lift up his countenance upon you, and give you peace.*

*Amen.*

# APPENDIX

STATE OF TEXAS
OFFICE OF THE GOVERNOR

GEORGE W. BUSH
GOVERNOR

February 13, 1998

Mr. Robert B. Eldredge, Sr.
428 Los Altos Way, Suite 203
Altamonte Springs, FL 32714

Dear Mr. Eldredge:

Thank you for your letter about Karla Faye Tucker.

When I was sworn in as the Governor of Texas, I took an oath of office to uphold the laws of our state, including the death penalty. My responsibility is to make sure our laws are enforced fairly and evenly without preference or special treatment. According to the Texas Constitution, the Governor may only commute a sentence if the Texas Board of Pardons and Paroles recommends it. Because the 18-member Board denied commutation in this case, my only independent authority as Governor was to grant a one-time 30-day stay of execution.

Many people have contacted my office about this execution. I respect the strong convictions that have prompted some to call for mercy and others to emphasize accountability and consequences. Like many touched by this case, I sought guidance through prayer. I concluded that judgments about the heart and soul of an individual on death row are best left to a higher authority.

Karla Faye Tucker acknowledged she was guilty of a horrible crime. She was convicted and sentenced by a jury of her peers. The role of the state is to enforce our laws and make sure all individuals are treated fairly under those laws. The state must make sure each individual sentenced to death has opportunity for access to the courts and thorough legal review. The courts, including the United States Supreme Court, reviewed the legal issues in this case; therefore, I did not grant a 30-day delay.

My prayers are with Karla Faye Tucker, her victims and their families.

Sincerely,

GEORGE W. BUSH

GWB:mg

You Can Also Read Robert Eldredge Sr.'s book on
Marriage!

*Christian Divorce, Christian Remarriage:*
*Your Practical Guide to the Born Again*
*Marriage*

Is available at

Choicepublications.org

Breathofalmighty.org

Amazon,

Barnes & Noble

Booksellers around the globe!